# SPRACHENZERTIFIKAT
# ENGLISCH B1

Common European Framework B1



## Übungsaufgaben im Stil der Prüfung

mit Audio-CD

STARK

**Bildnachweis**
Umschlag (von links nach rechts): © Debra James/Dreamstime.com; © Barbiedohl/Dreamstime.com; © Matthijs Rijken/www.sxc.hu
S. 1: © Seesea/Dreamstime.com
S. 9: © Niko Fagerström/www.dreamstime.com
S. 12 unten: © Andres Rodriguez/Dreamstime.com
S. 13 (von oben nach unten): © Andres Rodriguez/Dreamstime.com; © Kaarsten/Dreamstime.com; © Enigmatico/Dreamstime.com; © Vinicius Tupinamba/dreamstime.com; © Simon Krzic I Dreamstime.com
S. 14 Geige: © Sergey Goruppa/Dreamstime.com; Horrorfilme: © Atif Gulzar/sxc.hu, © Maciej Pawlik/sxc.hu; Dorset: http://commons. wikimedia.org/wiki/File: Bronkham_Hill_barrow_cemtery_dorset.jpg, Published under the terms of the GNU Free Documentation License, Version 1.2 or any later version published by the Free Software Foundation; Tennis: © Cybernesco/Dreamstime.com;
Kopfhörer: © Sergey Sizkov/Dreamstime.com; Gitarre: © Dreamstime/Guy Shapira
S. 16: © Luca Oleastri/Dreamstime.com
S. 17 Prince: Tim Mosenfelder/Getty Images; Madonna, Michael Jackson: AFP/Getty Images
S. 22 /36 (oben links nach unten rechts): © Dreamstime/Guy Shapira; © Rui Matos/Dreamstime.com; © Andres Rodriguez/Dreamstime.com; © Vassiliy Mikhailin/Dreamstime.com; © Spe/Dreamstime.com; © Robert Paul Van Beets/Dreamstime.com; © Bartlomiej Magierowski/Dreamstime.com; © Jimmy Lu/Dreamstime.com; © Alinoubigh/www.dreamstime.com; © Forsterfores/www.dreamstime.com
S. 23 /37 (oben links nach unten rechts): © Josep Altarriba/sxc.hu; © Andres Rodriguez/Dreamstime.com; © Boris Ryaposov/Dreamstime.com; © Andres Rodriguez/Dreamstime.com
S. 27: © Serghei Starus/Dreamstime.com; © Feng Yu/Dreamstime.com; © Henrischmit/Dreamstime.com; © Temistocle Lucarelli/Dreamstime.com; © Christopher Hall/Dreamstime.com; © Bartosz Ostrowski/Dreamstime.com; © Minh Tang/Dreamstime.com
S. 28 links: www.visipix.com; rechts: © Gh19/Dreamstime.com
S. 43 A /D: © Ch. Bartholmai; B/C: © Larry Kelly, www.manythings.org
S. 44 E: © Larry Kelly, www.manythings.org; F: http://commons.wikimedia.org/wiki/File:Neon_Internet_Cafe_open_24_hours.jpg; This file is licensed under the Creative Commons Attribution ShareAlike 2.0 License.; G /H: © Ch. Bartholmai
S. 46 links: © Raisa Kanareva/Dreamstime.com; rechts: © Photowitch/Dreamstime.com
S. 51/64 (oben links nach unten rechts): © photocase; http://commons.wikimedia.org/wiki/File:Lightning_NOAA.jpg; © Dmitryp/ Dreamstime.com; © Cammeraydave/Dreamstime.com
S. 52/64/65 (von links oben nach rechts unten): © Aleksandar Jocic/Dreamstime.com; © Xanya69/Dreamstime.com; © Nataliya Evmenenko/ Dreams¬time.com; © Maria Gritsai/Dreamstime.com; © Svyatoslav Palenyy/sxc.hu; © Yuriy Panyukov/Dreamstime.com; © Vuk Nenezic/Dreamstime.com; © Igor Terekhov/Dreamstime.com
S. 55 (links oben nach rechts unten): © Ron Sumners/Dreamstime.com; http://commons.wikimedia.org/wiki/File:Liberty-statue-from-below.jpg; http://commons.wikimedia.org/wiki/File:London_Big_Ben_Phone_box.jpg, This file is licensed under the Creative Commons Attribution ShareAlike 2.5 License.; © Christopher Bowers/Dreamstime.com
S. 56 links: KNS/AFP/Getty Images; rechts: http://commons.wikimedia.org/wiki/File:BarackObamaportrait.jpg
S. 73: © Barbara Riescher
S. 74: © Jorge Aguilera/sxc.hu
S. 79/92 (oben links nach unten rechts): © Oleksandr Kalyna/Dreamstime.com; © Tad Denson/Dreamstime.com; © Rainer Claus/Fotolia.de; © Franz Pfluegl/Dreamstime.com; © Jean Scheijen/sxc.hu; © sanja gjenero/sxc.hu
S. 80/93 (oben links nach unten rechts): © Vitaliy Rozhkov/Dreamstime.com; http://commons.wikimedia.org/wiki/File:Kapsylparken.JPG; This file is licensed under the Creative Commons Attribution 3.0 Unported License.; © kliverap/sxc.hu; http://commons.wikimedia.org/wiki/File:Round¬about. bristol. arp.jpg; © Ioachim Gherman/www.sxc.hu; © Feng Yu/Dreamstime.com; © Jean Scheijen/sxc.hu
S. 83 (oben links nach unten rechts): © Nikolay Mamluke/Dreamstime.com; © Fallenangel/Dreamstime.com; © Yuri Arcurs/Dreamstime.com; © Ned White/Dreamstime.com; © Carl Durocher/Dreamstime.com; © Popa Sorin/Dreamstime.com
S. 84 links: © Alexey Efanov/Dreamstime.com; rechts: © Alexander Yakovlev/Dreamstime.com
S. 101: © Suljo/Dreamstime.com
S. 102: http://commons.wikimedia.org/wiki/File:Alcatraz_pano_MC.jpg; This file is licensed under Creative Commons Attribution 2.5 License
S. 106 links und rechts: © Jean Scheijen/sxc.hu; Mitte: Redaktion
S. 107/118/119 (oben links nach unten rechts): © Christoph Weihs/Dreamstime.com; http://commons.wikimedia.org/wiki/File:Og%C3%B3rki…jpg; This file is licensed under the Creative Commons Attribution ShareAlike 3.0 License.; © Alesandra Przenioslo/sxc.hu; © Jean Scheijen/sxc.hu; © Nikolaev/Dreams¬time.com; © Agata Urbaniak/sxc.hu; © Michal Zacharzewski/sxc.hu; © Josep Altarriba/sxc.hu
S. 108/119: © Bruce Parrott/Dreamstime.com; © Oksana Tumeniuk/Dreamstime.com; © Chucky/Dreamstime.com
S. 110 (oben links nach unten rechts): © Absolut_photos/Dreamstime.com; © Chode/Dreamstime.com; © Michal Adamczyk/Dreamstime.com; © Vadkoz/Dreamstime.com; © Marc Dietrich/Dreamstime.com; © Joao Virissimo/Dreamstime.com
S. 111 links: © Oleg Gerasymenko/Dreamstime.com; rechts: © Otnaydur/Dreamstime.com
S. 126 A: http://commons.wikimedia.org/wiki/File:Kingston_park_and_ride_advert_Ede[illegible].JPG; This file is licensed under the Creative Commons Attribution ShareAlike 3.0 License. C: © Michel Meynsbrughen/sxc.hu D: © So[illegible]hison/Dreamstime.com
E: © Mailthepic/Dreamstime.com; G: http://commons.wikimedia.org/wiki/File:Playa_Acces[illegible]svg; H: © Gözde Otman/sxc.hu
S. 127: © Lorna/Dreamstime.com
S. 128: © Noam Armonn/Dreamstime.com
S. 133/145/146 (oben links nach unten rechts): © Nyul/Dreamstime.com; © Kristian Sekulic/Dreamstime.com; © Richardforeman/Dreamstime.com; © Michael Shake/Dreamstime.com; © Kriss Szkurlatowski/sxc.hu; © Ali Taylor/sxc.hu; © Lisa F. Young/Dreamstime.com; © Sean Locke/iStockphoto.com; © Elena Kouptsova-vasic/Dreamstime.com
S. 134/146 (oben links nach unten rechts): © Bryan Creely/Dreamstime.com; © Rainer Claus/Fotolia.de; © Viatcheslav Dusaleev/Dreamstime.com; © Mchudo/Dreamstime.com; © Dragan Trifunovic/Dreamstime.com; © Marie-claude Lapointe/Dreamstime.com; © Helenbird/Dreamstime.com; © Annie Su Yee Yek/Dreamstime.com
S. 137 (oben links nach unten rechts): © Monkey Business Images/Dreams¬time.com; © Willeecole/Dreamstime.com; © Kmitu/Dreamstime.com; © Vivek Gupta/sxc.hu; © BSK/sxc.hu; http://commons.wikimedia.org/wiki/File:Frederic_Remington_smoke_signal.jpg
S. 138 links: © Cinetext/Sight of Sound; rechts: © Cinetext/Distler

ISBN 978-3-86668-154-5

# Inhalt



**Autor:**
Patrick Charles

# Vorwort

## Liebe Schülerin, lieber Schüler,

der Erwerb eines international anerkannten Sprachenzertifikats gewinnt immer mehr an Bedeutung. Die Anforderungen bei einer solchen Prüfung sind standardisiert, d. h. man kann so Leistungen und Kenntnisse länderübergreifend vergleichen. Anders als bei der Abschlussprüfung an der Schule, wo die Ergebnisse nur innerhalb eines Bundeslandes verglichen werden können, gelten für die Sprachenzertifikats-Prüfungen in ganz Europa einheitliche Anforderungen. Eine erfolgreiche Teilnahme gilt somit als europaweiter Sprachkompetenznachweis, da sich die Zuordnung der Sprachenzertifikate an den Niveaustufen des Gemeinsamen Europäischen Referenzrahmens (GER) orientiert. Für das Zertifikat auf das dieser Band vorbereitet (z. B. PET oder telc B 1) ist es das Niveau B 1.

Speziell als Ergänzung zu einem Schulabschluss oder um sich bei einer Bewerbung für einen Praktikums-, Ausbildungs- oder Arbeitsplatz von anderen Kandidaten abzuheben, lohnt sich der Einsatz auf jeden Fall. Plant man einen längeren Aufenthalt im Ausland, so empfiehlt es sich ebenfalls, einen international anerkannten Nachweis für Sprachkenntnisse mitzubringen. Mit einem Zertifikat weisen Sie nach, dass Sie in allen Kompetenzbereichen *(Reading, Language Elements, Writing, Listening und Speaking)* über im Alltag einsetzbare Kenntnisse verfügen.

Die folgenden Tipps und Hinweise sowie die fünf *Mock Exams* – Aufgaben die sich ganz genau am Stil der Prüfung orientieren – sollen Ihnen helfen, Ihre Prüfung für das Sprachenzertifikat B 1 erfolgreich zu meistern.

### Wie sieht der Test aus?

Der Test gliedert sich in vier bzw. fünf Teile, je nach Prüfungsanbieter variiert der Aufbau geringfügig. Beispielsweise können Aufgaben zu ***Language Elements*** (Wortschatz und Grammatik) auch in die Bereiche *Reading* und *Writing* integriert sein. Bei ***Reading*** erwarten Sie meist Multiple Choice Aufgaben oder Zuordnungsaufgaben, die das Textverständnis abprüfen.

Offenere Frage finden Sie im Bereich ***Writing***. Hier müssen Sie eine kurze Mitteilung, eine E-Mail oder einen Brief verfassen oder eine Geschichte zu Ende schreiben. Je nach Anbieter stehen Ihnen für die Prüfungsteile *Reading, Language Elements* und *Writing* zwischen 90 und 120 Minuten zur Verfügung.

Der Prüfungsteil ***Listening*** dauert ca. 30 Minuten und hier kommen alle Arbeitsanweisungen von der CD. Sie gibt Ihnen auch die genaue Zeit vor, die für die einzelnen Aufgaben zur Verfügung steht. Alle Texte werden zweimal vorgespielt, also keine Sorge, wenn Sie beim ersten Hören nicht gleich alles verstehen.

Bitte denken Sie unbedingt daran, dass Sie bei der schriftlichen Prüfung alle Antworten noch auf den **Antwortbogen** übertragen müssen. Bei manchen Anbietern steht Ihnen dafür keine zusätzliche Zeit mehr zur Verfügung.

Der ***Speaking***-Teil findet meist für zwei Prüfungskandidaten gemeinsam statt und dauert etwa 10 bis 12 Minuten. Er besteht aus vier Teilen, in denen

Sie z. T. alleine sprechen müssen, z. T. müssen Sie ein Gespräch mit einem Partner führen.
Sie finden auf den folgenden Seiten genauere Hinweise zu möglichen Aufgabenformen in allen Kompetenzbereichen. Machen Sie sich mit diesen vertraut und sehen Sie sich auch den kompletten Testablauf in diesem Buch an. So wissen Sie genau, was Sie in der Prüfung erwartet.
Der Prüfungsinhalt besteht vorwiegend aus kurzen Gebrauchstexten aus dem Alltag und etwas längeren Texten in alltäglichem Englisch. Üben Sie neben dem Unterricht mit einfachen Zeitungsartikeln, Kleinanzeigen, Werbung, Hinweistafeln, Gebrauchsanweisungen, Formularen, Packungsbeilagen, Fahrplänen etc. Wenn Sie z. B. ein Formular im Internet ausfüllen, sehen Sie sich wenn möglich auch die englische Version an.

**Wie kann man mit diesem Buch arbeiten?**

In diesem Buch erhalten Sie einige allgemeine Hinweise und Tipps zur Bearbeitung Ihrer Sprachenzertifikats-Prüfung. Im Anschluss daran finden Sie fünf *Mock Exams*, mit denen Sie sich optimal auf die Aufgabenformen der Prüfung vorbereiten können. Hier können Sie den Ernstfall proben.
Sehen Sie sich zuerst die Erklärungen zu den einzelnen Prüfungsteilen an, damit Sie wissen, worum es bei den jeweiligen Aufgaben geht und wie sie zu bearbeiten sind.

Sie können auf unterschiedliche Weise mit diesem Buch arbeiten.

Möglichkeit 1

Sie machen zuerst als Test ein *Mock Exam* und vergleichen danach Ihre Antworten mit der Musterlösung. So sehen Sie, wo Ihre Stärken liegen und wo Sie noch etwas mehr üben müssen. Bearbeiten Sie danach gezielt Aufgaben zu den Bereichen, die Ihnen Probleme bereiten. Sie können sich beim Üben ruhig mehr Zeit nehmen als in der Prüfung. Auch die Hörtexte können Sie sich so oft anhören wie es für Sie hilfreich ist. Wiederholen Sie nach einiger Zeit die *Mock Exams* unter Testbedingungen.

Möglichkeit 2

Wenn Sie sich schon relativ sicher fühlen, üben Sie mit den *Mock Exams* unter „realen Bedingungen“, d. h. unter Einhaltung der entsprechenden Zeitvorgaben, damit Sie einschätzen können, wo Ihre Stärken und Schwächen liegen bzw. wie lange Sie für die einzelnen Aufgaben benötigen. Vergleichen Sie Ihre Antworten mit den Lösungen und wiederholen Sie die *Mock Exams* gegebenenfalls nach einiger Zeit. Natürlich können Sie sich die Zeit selbst einteilen, d. h. Sie beginnen mit den Aufgaben, die Ihnen üblicherweise am besten gelingen oder die Sie am schnellsten bearbeiten können.

Nutzen Sie in jedem Fall die Vorlagen der ***Answer sheets*** im beiliegenden Heft und üben Sie auch das Übertragen. So sind Sie in der Prüfung routiniert, müssen nicht auf den Bögen herumsuchen und gewinnen wertvolle Zeit. Es zählen nur Ihre Antworten, die Sie auch tatsächlich auf dem Antwortbogen eingetragen haben.

**Weitere praktische Tipps**

- Lassen Sie keinesfalls Aufgaben unbeantwortet, sondern verlassen Sie sich im Zweifelsfall auf Ihr „Bauchgefühl“. Bevor Sie gar nichts hinschreiben, raten Sie bei Multiple Choice Aufgaben lieber. So haben Sie noch eine gewisse Chance auf die richtige Lösung.
- Üben Sie immer wieder das Buchstabieren von Namen und Begriffen; das kommt Ihnen sowohl im *Listening-* als auch im *Speaking*-Teil der Prüfung zu Gute.
- Halten Sie sich immer genau an die Aufgabenstellung *(write one to three words, write 35–45 words etc.)*. Sollten Sie sich nicht mehr sicher sein, finden Sie die Arbeitsanweisung immer am Anfang der Aufgabe.
- Arbeiten Sie ruhig und konzentriert, ohne zu viele Pausen einzulegen. Vor der Abschlusskontrolle und der Übertragung der Lösungen auf den Antwortbogen sollten Sie sich aber eine kurze Auszeit gönnen. So bekommen Sie den Kopf wieder frei und können mögliche Fehler gezielt korrigieren.
- Verwenden Sie für das Ausfüllen der *Answer sheets* einen weichen Bleistift (Härtegrad B oder HB) und markieren Sie das richtige Kästchen. Beachten Sie, dass Sie die Kästchen nicht ankreuzen sollen, sondern komplett ausfüllen müssen. Wenn Sie eine Antwort ändern möchten, radieren Sie diese aus und stellen Sie sicher, dass Ihre Antworten gut lesbar sind.
- Achten Sie beim Übertragen Ihrer Lösungen immer darauf, dass Ihre Antwort neben der richtigen Aufgabennummer auf dem Antwortbogen steht.

Und nun wünsche ich Ihnen viel Spaß beim Bearbeiten der *Mock Exams* und vor allem viel Erfolg in Ihrer Prüfung!

Ihr

Patrick Charles

## ▶ Hinweise und Tipps zum Sprachenzertifikat B 1

## Hinweise und Tipps

### *Reading*

In diesem Bereich begegnen Ihnen unterschiedliche **Textsorten**. Es kommen oft kurze Gebrauchstexte wie eine Packungsbeilage, eine Gebrauchsanweisung, ein Auszug aus einem Bestellformular, Hinweis- oder Verkehrsschilder vor. Außerdem sollen Sie auch etwas längere Texte bewältigen, wie z. B. Zeitungsartikel, Werbung oder ausführlichere Stellenangebote.
Während es bei den Textsorten eine etwas größere Bandbreite gibt, werden Ihnen in den einzelnen Prüfungsteilen immer wieder die gleichen **Aufgabentypen** begegnen. Meist steht am Anfang ein Beispiel (0), das Ihnen zeigt, was zu tun ist.

*multiple choice*

Hier müssen Sie aus drei oder vier Antwortmöglichkeiten die richtige auswählen. Sehen Sie sich die Auswahlmöglichkeiten genau an. Häufig kommen ähnliche Begriffe oder auch gleiche Wörter vor, der Sinn ist aber unterschiedlich. Prüfen Sie immer den Inhalt der Aussage und vergleichen Sie diese mit der Textstelle, auf die sie sich bezieht. Sobald Sie meinen die richtige Antwort gefunden zu haben, wägen Sie noch einmal ab, ob es eine noch genauer zutreffende Lösung gibt.

Beispiel

☐ **A** *Large trucks, lorries or buses must drive in the middle of the road when they cross the bridge.*

☑ **B** *Large trucks, lorries and buses must drive in the centre of the road.*

☐ **C** *A bridge is being built over the road.*

Lückentext mit *multiple choice*

Auswahlantworten begegnen Ihnen auch bei Lückentexten. Sie müssen hier aus vier Möglichkeiten die richtige auswählen *(four-option multiple-choice cloze)*. Beachten Sie, dass es immer nur eine richtige Lösung gibt. Das Wort bzw. die Wendung muss sich sowohl grammatikalisch als auch inhaltlich gut in den Text einfügen. Diese Aufgabe wird je nach Anbieter auch dem Bereich *Language Elements* zugeordnet.

Beispiel

*My name is Pwyll, which is (0) ________ for "Paul".*

**A** ☐ *Wales* **B** ☐ *Whales* **C** ☑ *Welsh* **D** ☐ *Welch* *matching*

Ihnen werden fünf kurze Texte (z. B. Beschreibungen von Personen) vorgelegt. Außerdem erhalten Sie acht weitere Texte (z. B. Stellenangebote), aus denen Sie fünf auswählen und den ersten Texten zuordnen müssen. Sie vergleichen also, welche Stelle zu welcher Person passen würde und wählen die entsprechenden Texte aus. Ein Stellenangebot kann aber immer nur einer Person zugeordnet werden und einige passen zu keiner Person.

*true/false*

Hier müssen Sie entscheiden, ob eine Aussage auf den Text zutrifft oder nicht. Suchen Sie im Text nach Schlüsselwörtern und vergleichen Sie die entsprechende Stelle mit der Aussage. Lesen Sie genau, oft enthält das Statement zwar ähnliche Wörter, entspricht aber doch nicht dem Sinn des Texts.

Beispiel

*Everybody loves Australia, with its huge landscapes, small population and amazing natural wonders. It's also a brilliant place to work and travel, and we offer guaranteed work there for up to a year.*

*After reading the text, decide if the statements are true or false.*
*Tick (✓) **A** for **true** or **B** for **false**.*

| | A | B |
|---|---|---|
| *The agency offers work in Australia for a maximum of 12 months.* | ☑ | ☐ |

## *Writing*

In diesem Prüfungsteil müssen Sie oft zunächst Aufgaben bearbeiten, bei denen Sie vorgegebenen Text paraphrasieren müssen. Anschließend folgen weitere Aufgaben, bei denen Sie selbst kurze Texte verfassen müssen

*sentence transformation*

Sie bekommen einen Satz vorgelegt und sollen einen zweiten Satz so ergänzen, dass er den gleichen Sinn ergibt wie der erste. Beachten Sie, dass Sie nur ein bis drei Wörter verwenden dürfen um die Lücke zu füllen. Übertragen Sie auch nur diese Wörter auf ihr Antwortblatt.

Beispiel

*My car was repaired last weekend.*
*I __had my__ car fixed last weekend.*

*write*

Daneben werden Ihnen bei *Writing* auch noch offenere Aufgaben gestellt, bei denen Sie einen kurzen Text schreiben sollen. Manchmal dürfen Sie auch zwischen zwei verschiedenen Aufgaben auswählen. Häufig wird Ihnen eine Situation vorgegeben und Sie müssen bestimmte Informationen in einer SMS, einer E-Mail, einem Blog, etc. weitergeben. Lesen Sie hier die Aufgabenstellung besonders gründlich und achten Sie darauf, alle geforderten Aspekte in Ihren Text aufzunehmen. Etwas freier sind Sie bei Aufgaben, wo Ihnen der erste Satz vorgegeben wird und Sie eine kurze Geschichte schreiben sollen.

Im Bereich *Writing* können Sie eine Bewertung zwischen 0 (absolut unverständlich) und maximal 5 (alle Aspekte klar verständlich, nur minimale Grammatik- und Rechtschreibfehler) erzielen. Ihr Text muss nicht perfekt sein, aber den allgemeinen Regeln (z. B. Anrede und Abschlussformel einer E-Mail/eines Briefs) entsprechen. Benutzen Sie nur Wörter und Wendungen, die Sie sicher beherrschen und schreiben Sie kurze, einfache Sätze. Überlegen Sie nicht zu lange, sollte Ihnen ein Wort nicht einfallen. Versuchen Sie lieber zu umschreiben, was Sie sagen möchten. Halten Sie sich bei allen Aufgaben unbedingt an die geforderte Anzahl von Wörtern. Zu kurze Texte müssen schlechter bewertet werden. Auch wenn Ihr Text länger ist als gefordert riskieren Sie eine schlechtere Bewertung, da einige inhaltliche Aspekte eventuell nicht relevant sind oder Ihr Text mehr Fehler enthält.

## *Listening*

Auch beim Hörverstehen werden Sie mit Texten unterschiedlicher Länge und aus verschiedenen Bereichen konfrontiert. Häufig kommen **Ansagen** (z. B. am Bahnhof, im Flugzeug, im Supermarkt, auf dem Anrufbeantworter) oder kurze **Alltagsdialoge** vor. Außerdem gibt es Aufgaben zu **längeren Monologen** oder **Dialogen** (z. B. Radiosendung, Interview, Podcast, Gespräche zwischen Freunden).

*multiple choice*

Wie beim Leseverstehen müssen Sie hier eine von drei Antwortmöglichkeiten aussuchen. Oft gibt es auch Multiple Choice Aufgaben mit Bildern, d. h. Sie wählen das passende Bild aus. Kreuzen Sie schon beim ersten Zuhören die Antwort an, die Sie für richtig halten und versuchen Sie beim zweiten Durchgang auf Einzelheiten zu achten, die Ihnen noch für die Lösung der Aufgaben fehlen. Häufig werden mehrere in den Lösungen vorkommende Wörter erwähnt. Lesen Sie die Frage nochmals genau durch und versuchen Sie beim zweiten Mal, die beste Lösung zu finden. Sollten Sie etwas auch beim zweiten Hören nicht verstanden haben, versuchen Sie die Lösung aus dem Zusammenhang zu erschließen. Oft hilft Ihnen logisches Kombinieren auch weiter.

*gap-fill*

Bei dieser Aufgabe sollen Sie in einen Lückentext oder in einer Tabelle Informationen aus dem Hörtext eintragen. Vorsicht, der Wortlaut dieses Texts entspricht nicht dem Hörtext. Es sind hier oft mehrere Lösungen richtig, Sie müssen sich allerdings für eine Variante entscheiden und diese in ihr *Answer sheet* übertragen.

Beispiel

*Listening text: Here's the weather report for travellers in Britain today. The south and west is looking forward to some great weather today, lots of sun and summery temperatures. Things get a bit colder the further north we go, and Scotland is going to have to get ready for some stormy weather later today, with strong winds and heavy rains from the Highlands down to Newcastle.*

*Weather forecast for:*
- *the south of England:* sunny, warm
- *the Scottish Highlands:* storm, rain

*true/false*

Hier müssen Sie wieder Aussagen zum Text überprüfen und entscheiden, ob sie richtig oder falsch sind (vgl. Beispiel zu *Reading*). Markieren Sie auch hier schon während des ersten Hörens die Antworten, die für Sie eindeutig sind. Konzentrieren Sie sich beim zweiten Hören auf die Stellen, die Ihnen noch fehlen. Manchmal können Sie Antworten auch aus dem Gesamtkontext erschließen.

Je nach Anbieter haben Sie am Ende des Prüfungsteils *Listening* noch Zeit Ihre Antworten in das *Answer sheet* einzutragen.

## *Speaking*

mögliche Aufgaben

Der *Speaking*-Teil dauert etwa 10 bis 12 Minuten und besteht aus drei bis vier Teilen. Im **ersten Teil**, einem kurzen Interview, stellt der Prüfer einige persönliche Fragen. Sie sollten Auskunft geben können über alltägliche Dinge wie z. B.:
- Ihren Namen (den Sie meist auch buchstabieren müssen),
- Wohnort,
- Familie,
- Schule/Berufsleben,
- Hobbies/Interessen,
- Freizeit/Urlaub.

Sie können auch aufgefordert werden, sich gegenseitig Fragen zu diesen Themen zu stellen. In diesem Fall erhalten Sie ein *candidate sheet* mit möglichen Aspekten, nach denen Sie fragen können. Achten Sie darauf, nicht stur diese Liste abzuarbeiten, sondern ein möglichst natürliches Gespräch zu führen, um den anderen kennen zu lernen.
Denken Sie daran, dass Ihre Antworten nicht unbedingt der Wahrheit entsprechen müssen. Wenn Ihnen gerade das Wort für Ihren Lieblingssport oder ein Leibgericht nicht einfällt, dann nehmen Sie einfach etwas anderes. Es kommt in erster Linie darauf an, das Gespräch authentisch fortzuführen. Geben Sie so viele Informationen wie möglich, auch wenn Sie sonst vielleicht eher schüchtern sind.

Im **zweiten Teil** wird Ihnen beispielsweise eine Situation vorgestellt und Sie erhalten dazu passende Bilder. Der Prüfer wiederholt die Arbeitsanweisungen noch einmal und dann führen Sie ein Gespräch mit Ihrem Partner.
Bei einer weiteren Aufgabenform (im **zweiten** oder **dritten Prüfungsteil**) erhalten beide Kandidaten unterschiedliche Bilder, manchmal in Verbindung mit Zitaten oder Fragen. Jeder Kandidat beschreibt sein Bild für den Partner und spricht zunächst alleine über das Thema. Danach folgt ein gemeinsames Gespräch darüber.
Bei einer Variante dieser Aufgabe spricht jeder Kandidat nur alleine über sein Thema, der Partner hört zu. An diese Aufgabe kann sich ein **weiterer Prüfungsteil** anschließen, in dem sich jeder Kandidat zusammenfassend über beide Bilder äußern muss.
In einem **weiteren Prüfungsteil** kann von Ihnen verlangt werden, dass Sie sich nach einigen inhaltlichen Vorgaben auf ein gemeinsames Ziel einigen sollen. Sie verabreden sich beispielsweise für das Wochenende und vereinbaren, was Sie machen wollen und wann und wo Sie sich treffen wollen.

Ablauf und Bewertung

Ob Ihnen für den *Speaking*-Teil eine Vorbereitungszeit gewährt wird, hängt vom Anbieter der Prüfung ab. Es werden meist zwei Kandidaten zusammen geprüft. Einer der Prüfer unterhält sich mit Ihnen, der zweite hört zu. Sie bekommen vor der mündlichen Prüfung *Mark sheets*, zur Weitergabe an die Prüfer. Sie brauchen auf den *Mark sheets* nichts einzutragen; geben Sie sie einfach auf Verlangen an den Prüfer. Versuchen Sie die Fragen so genau wie möglich zu beantworten und immer zu begründen. Wenn Ihnen ein Wort fehlt, ersetzen Sie es durch einen ähnlichen Begriff oder umschreiben Sie es und sprechen einfach weiter. Neben Vokabelkenntnissen, Grammatik und Aussprache wird auch bewertet, wie gut Sie mit Ihrem Partner bzw. dem Prüfer zusammenarbeiten bzw. ob Sie versuchen die Fragen zu beantworten, um zu einem Ergebnis zu kommen.
Beide Kandidaten werden getrennt voneinander von beiden Prüfern anhand der Vorgaben für das Prüfungsniveau B 1 bewertet. Der Prüfer mit dem Sie sprechen, gibt Ihnen eine Gesamtnote, während der beisitzende Prüfer Grammatik und Vokabelkenntnisse, Aussprache, *Discourse Management* (sinnvoller Zusammenhang des Gesagten, Bezug zur Fragestellung) und *Interactive Communication* (Fähigkeit ein Gespräch in Gang zu bringen bzw. zu halten, Zusammenspiel mit dem Gesprächspartner) bewertet. Es geht hier in erster Linie darum, Ihre sprachlichen Fähigkeiten zu testen, eine inhaltliche Vollständigkeit bei der Beantwortung der Fragen ist nicht so wichtig.

Tipps und hilfreiche Wendungen

Üben Sie vorher, wenn möglich mit einem Partner, das nimmt Ihnen die Nervosität und bereitet Sie optimal vor. Arbeiten Sie immer wieder mit den Bildimpulsen aus diesem Buch.

Achten Sie bei Prüfungsteilen, bei denen Sie mit einem Partner sprechen darauf, dass jeder zu Wort kommt. Stellen Sie Fragen und gehen Sie auf das ein, was Ihr Partner sagt. Folgende Wendungen sollten Sie sich merken:

- *What do you think about …? What is your opinion about …?*
- *Do you agree with …?*
- *I think you're absolutely right. Let me just add that …*
- *Don't you think that …?*
- *Sorry, but I disagree. I think you're totally wrong here.*
- *Are you saying that …?*
- *Sorry to interrupt, but I would like to add that …*

Fällt Ihnen einmal nicht gleich etwas ein, so können Ihnen diese „Füllwörter" helfen, etwas Zeit zum Nachdenken zu gewinnen:

- *Well.*
- *Let me see.*
- *I'm not sure, but …*
- *I mean …*
- *Look …*
- *What I'm trying to say is …*
- *Do you see what I mean? / … if you see what I mean.*

Bei vielen Aufgaben erhalten Sie Bildimpulse. Hier sind einige Wendungen, die Sie benötigen, um darauf Bezug zu nehmen:

- *In the picture on the right-hand side / left-hand side you can see …*
- *The picture in the middle shows …*
- *The next one expresses a rather different aspect.*
- *In the foreground / background / centre …*
- *Looking at these pictures I think … The picture reminds me of …*
- *The mood conveyed in the picture is …*
- *The two pictures show very different forms of …*
- *The two pictures express opposing attitudes.*

## ▶ Übungsaufgaben im Stil des Sprachenzertifikats B 1

**Sprachenzertifikat Englisch B1**
***Mock Exam* 1**

## Reading

### Part 1

*Read the texts and choose the correct explanation.*
*Tick (✓) the correct sentences and mark the letter (A–C) on your answer sheet.*
*There is an example at the beginning (0).*

0.

- [x] **A** Large trucks, lorries and buses must drive in the centre of the road.
- [ ] **B** Large trucks, lorries or buses must drive in the middle of the road when they cross the bridge.
- [ ] **C** A bridge is being built over the road.

1.

**ALFREDO'S RESTAURANT**
will be closed
**from July 23rd**
**to August 14th**
due to repairs in the kitchens and redecoration in the dining areas. We apologise for the inconvenience, and wish our guests a happy summer!
**The Management**

- [ ] **A** The restaurant is going to close for the summer because there are no customers.
- [ ] **B** Alfredo's is going to look different when it opens again later in the summer.
- [ ] **C** The restaurant will be closed for over a month while the kitchens are being repaired.

2.

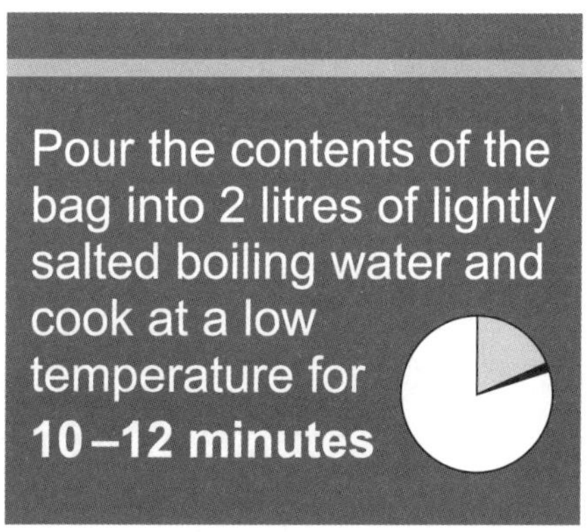


- [ ] **A** The contents must be poured into water and then brought to the boil for 10–12 minutes.
- [ ] **B** The contents should be poured into boiling water and then kept on a low heat.
- [ ] **C** Pour salt into boiling water and cook for 10–12 minutes before adding the contents of the bag.

3.

- [ ] **A** Passengers must bring at least two pieces of luggage with them when they come on board.
- [ ] **B** Passengers must store all their luggage in the space above their seat or under their seat.
- [ ] **C** Travellers can only bring two pieces of hand luggage with them, and these must be carefully stored under the seat in front of them or in the space above their seat.

4.

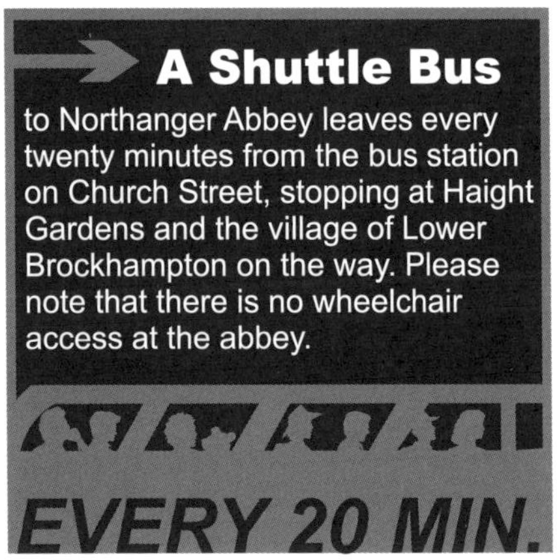


- [ ] **A** The bus journey takes twenty minutes and makes three stops.
- [ ] **B** Visitors in wheelchairs will need help when they get to the abbey.
- [ ] **C** The abbey is on the way to the village of Lower Brockhampton.

## Part 2

*Buying Christmas presents: Match the people (5–9) to the presents (A–H).*
*Maybe not everyone is going to get a present this year …*

5. Grandma Wilkinson

I like to read, I enjoy historical romances and books about the history of the area where I grew up. I also like cookery books.

6. Robert

*I got an X-Box 360 for my birthday this year and I would like some new games for it, I also enjoy playing tennis and would like a new racquet.*

7. Cordelia's brother

*I've just started taking violin lessons, and my brother would really like some ear plugs for Christmas ....*

8. Mr Wilkinson

*I would like to read more about the Mafia and organised crime in general.*

9. Mrs Wilkinson

*I would most like a DVD of one of my favourite films. I most like films based on English literature, but I also enjoy romantic comedies.*

A
4-CD box
Nigel Kennedy
FAMOUS VIOLIN PIECES
NIGEL KENNEDY
1
2
3
4
B
Charles Dickens
five great novels
10 CD/DVD
C
DESTROYER'S PARADISE XXI
Grave of Sudden Death VIII
Night of FLESH-EATING ZOMBIES III
D
Learn Italian in 2 Weeks
E
for quiet moments
Luxury
F
Dorset through the Ages
A Nostalgic Journey in Photographs
by The Dorset Historical Society
G
GRAND SLAM
How Organised Crime Has Changed The Face of Tennis
by Luigi Benanotti
H
Guitar Lessons
- Beginners and experts -
teacher for classical, rock and jazz guitar
call Pete on 446565

| 5 | 6 | 7 | 8 | 9 |
|---|---|---|---|---|
| | | | | |

## Part 3

*After reading the text about alien languages, decide if the statements are true or false.*
*Tick (✓)* ***A*** *for* ***true*** *and* ***B*** *for* ***false****.*
*Mark the correct letter on your answer sheet.*

| | A | B |
|---|---|---|
| 10. The American scientist Dr. John Elliott has developed a computer programme which will help us understand alien languages. | ☐ | ☐ |
| 11. Over 60 human languages are included in the database which the software uses to analyse signals from outer space. | ☐ | ☐ |
| 12. Scientists are now able to listen to unknown signals and find out if they contain images, musical elements or language. | ☐ | ☐ |
| 13. The software will be able to translate different types of words. | ☐ | ☐ |
| 14. Dr. Elliott says that the project is very difficult because not all languages follow patterns. | ☐ | ☐ |
| 15. Because aliens are so much more intelligent than humans, there is very little chance of us being able to understand their languages. | ☐ | ☐ |
| 16. Dr. Elliott's software is designed to be able to analyse at least the structure of alien languages, even if it won't be able to understand what is being said. | ☐ | ☐ |
| 17. The database of over 60 human languages will be used to try to talk to the aliens, in the hope that they will understand at least some of our human languages. | ☐ | ☐ |
| 18. British scientists don't believe that it is possible that Dr. Elliott's software will ever work. | ☐ | ☐ |
| 19. American scientists are interested in Dr. Elliott's work and are very supportive. | ☐ | ☐ |

**Scientists are working on a computer programme to understand alien languages**

A British scientist is developing a computer programme which he believes will be able to identify and even translate languages from aliens in outer space.

The project started because scientists are worried that, even if humans do one day find alien life in space, we won't be able to understand what they say. Dr. John Elliott of Leeds Metropolitan University claims that the software he is helping to develop will be able to analyse and explain at least the structure of an alien language. This, he says, will be the most important first step in learning to understand aliens. He has compiled a database of over 60 human languages and is using this data to write his programme. Dr. Elliott believes that all languages have recognisable patterns, which will allow scientists using his computer programme to unlock the secrets of alien communication. Researchers in recent years have discovered that it is possible to analyse unknown signals and learn whether they contain music, images or language.

Dr. Elliott's software will be able to go one step further, and identify actual sentences and individual words. He says that his software can analyse alien communication and provide information on how intelligent the aliens might be – the computer programme will be able to analyse the length of sentences and then estimate how complex the language is, giving an indication of the intelligence of the species using it. His theory is that, if the aliens are much cleverer than us, their sentences will be much

longer and more complex than is the case in English, for example. He even claims that his programme will be able to identify certain types of words, such as verbs, adjectives or nouns. Dr. Elliott's programme would listen to alien communications and then compare them with the database of over 60 human languages, searching for any similarities which would help analyse the alien language. Dr. Elliott does say that this is only a start – recognising elements of a language and actually understanding what is being said are two different things. But other scientists in America are intrigued by the possibilities, and are encouraging Dr. Elliott's research.

## Part 4

*Read the text and answer the questions.*
*For each question, mark the correct letter A, B, C or D on your answer sheet.*

### The Bright Young Things of '80s pop turn 50 – and beyond

In the past few years, pop stars like 50 Cent, Eminem, Amy Winehouse, Britney Spears and Marilyn Manson have set the standard for public scandals. Whether they are getting shot in mysterious gangland struggles, shaving their heads and forgetting to wear underpants, beating up their wives, or attacking Christianity while wearing antique women's underwear – these pop stars are the most dangerous, challenging, and exciting artists ever in the history of pop music. Or are they? Every new generation of pop fans needs a rebellious focus – and while Marilyn Manson may shock grandparents today, and Britney Spears may make fans of 'serious' music depressed at the low standards of modern pop, everybody needs to step back just a couple of decades and have a look at who ruled the pop charts in the 1980s. The pop royalty of the '80s went by the names Prince Nile Rodgers, Madonna Louise Veronica Ciccone, and Michael Jackson.

Between them they had an inescapable influence on the sounds, looks and attitudes that fascinated young people during the first true pop decade. They were the pop artists that parents couldn't understand – why was Prince so weird? Why did Michael Jackson make music videos with zombies and werewolves? Why was Madonna so rude to her father, and why was she always trying to provoke the Catholics? They talked about the things that interested kids and teenagers at the time. They were rebellious, and everything they did sounded *new* – no music that had come before sounded like Prince's *Purple Rain* or Jackson's *Thriller*. So it's pretty strange now to think that the year 2008 saw all three of them turning 50. And beyond. Michael Jackson died – mysteriously, of course – in 2009. By that time, all three of the pop leaders of the 1980s had lost a lot of what made them special, and particularly, had lost almost everything that once made them relevant to kids and youth culture.

Prince vanished into the Internet in the late 1990s; he became one of the first pop stars to understand how important the world wide web would become for musicians. One of the most important things about Prince as a pop star in the 1980s was certainly his weirdness – a tiny man with big hair who wore ridiculous purple clothes, always surrounded himself with women who were bigger than him, and made music that never sounded like other people's. This weirdness is what saved him as an artist in the 21st century – it's no longer rebellious, perhaps: but the rebellion of a pop star in his 20s is the individuality of a pop star who has just turned 50. Prince has continued to go his own way, and his loyal audience follows him.

Madonna on the other hand has stayed very public. She may seem more like a scary fitness trainer these days than a glittering pop princess, and she gets more attention for her private life than for the quality of her music, but she still does what she's been doing since her first hits in the early 1980s – changing her image and her music to reach the taste of the kids who go to clubs to dance and who buy the records which make the Top 10. She's changed from being the "Material Girl" to being pop music's "Iron Lady", and at 50 she's still trying to show young people how to dance and how to dress.

The strangest character of them all, Michael Jackson also suffered the most under the media attention. Jackson was never really a rebel in the way that Madonna was, but what he accomplished with his music was a small revolution. More than any other artist in modern music he managed to bring different kinds of black and white music together – soul, pop, funk, rock, disco. Nowadays, listening to songs from Justin Timberlake or Britney Spears, it's hard to imagine that this was not always the case – but none of the American pop music we have today would have been possible without albums like *Thriller* and *Bad*.

Maybe today's pop stars are rebels, and maybe their scandals and gossip-magazine adventures are good at annoying parents and adults: but remember to ask those same adults and parents what *their* parents thought about Madonna's *Like A Prayer* video, or Prince's 'Purple' period – you may be surprised at how these middle-aged pop stars shook the establishment all those years ago!

20. What is the author of the text doing?

**A** ☐ Wishing three 1980s pop stars a happy birthday.

**B** ☐ Explaining why Prince is so strange today.

**C** ☐ Giving a short overview of the development of three 1980s pop stars.

**D** ☐ Giving an objective look at pop music in the 1980s.

21. What do you think the author's attitude is to the pop stars mentioned?

**A** ☐ The author likes Prince more than the others.

**B** ☐ The author thinks that Michael Jackson and Madonna were the greatest pop stars of their time.

**C** ☐ The author thinks that Prince was too weird to be a good pop star.

**D** ☐ The author thinks that the quality of Madonna's music is still the same.

22. Does the author have an opinion about pop stars still making music when they're 50?

**A** ☐ The author thinks it's wrong and that they should stop embarrassing themselves.

**B** ☐ The author doesn't give a clear opinion on the subject.

**C** ☐ The author's opinion is that people can continue making music as long as they like.

**D** ☐ The author's attitude is that some pop stars can still perform when they're 50, but that most of them should stop earlier.

23. What impression of the 1980s do you get from the text?

**A** ☐ The author thinks the 1980s were a very important time for pop music.

**B** ☐ The 1980s were a decade of bad taste and poor music.

**C** ☐ They were a very wild and rebellious time in which teenagers fought against their parents.

**D** ☐ It was boring because there was no Internet.

24. Choose the summary (A, B, C or D) which best applies to the text.

**A** ☐ Being an individual and following your own instincts is a good way to keep the respect of your fans.

**B** ☐ If pop stars carry on making music and performing for too long they become boring; nobody wants to see them anymore.

**C** ☐ Pop music is for children and teenagers. Adults shouldn't be listening to it and they certainly shouldn't be performing it.

**D** ☐ The best way to stay successful and popular is to look at what people want you to do, and then to try to do exactly that.

## Language Elements

*Read the text. The gaps in the text can be filled using the words in the lists below. Choose the correct letter A, B, C or D for each gap. There is an example at the beginning (0).*

**Haunted Holiday Houses in England …**
**Jamaica Inn, Cornwall**

Made (0) _______ by British author Daphne du Maurier, this 250-year-old tavern is (1) _______ to a large collection of smuggling souvenirs and antiques. But (2) _______ dark, it's not smugglers that (3) _______ need to worry about. At the Jamaica Inn you will experience inexplicable sounds of wheels and horses' hooves in the courtyard, footsteps in empty (4) _______, and the ghost of a murder victim who calmly sits outside, deep in thought …

**Chillingham Castle, Northumberland**

Chillingham is famous for the moans and cries of the Blue Boy. His crying and moaning has been (5) _______ near a wall, behind which his bones were (6) _______, along with scraps of blue clothing, suggesting that he may (7) _______ buried alive there. Up on the tower stairs, the rustle and whisper of dresses can be heard from the restless spirit of Lady Mary Berkeley as she hopelessly (8) _______ for her husband, who (9) _______ off with her sister and left her to die, heartbroken and alone.

| | | | | | | | | |
|---|---|---|---|---|---|---|---|---|
| 0 | **A** | ☐ visited | **B** | ☐ known | **C** | ☑ famous | **D** | ☐ tourist |
| 1 | **A** | ☐ home | **B** | ☐ museum | **C** | ☐ filled | **D** | ☐ famous |
| 2 | **A** | ☐ since | **B** | ☐ after | **C** | ☐ on | **D** | ☐ at |
| 3 | **A** | ☐ the police | **B** | ☐ she | **C** | ☐ a visitor | **D** | ☐ guests |
| 4 | **A** | ☐ corridors | **B** | ☐ cupboards | **C** | ☐ beds | **D** | ☐ streets |
| 5 | **A** | ☐ seen | **B** | ☐ feared | **C** | ☐ listened | **D** | ☐ heard |
| 6 | **A** | ☐ researched | **B** | ☐ discovered | **C** | ☐ figured out | **D** | ☐ investigated |
| 7 | **A** | ☐ was | **B** | ☐ have being | **C** | ☐ has been | **D** | ☐ have been |
| 8 | **A** | ☐ searches | **B** | ☐ seeks | **C** | ☐ watches | **D** | ☐ look |
| 9 | **A** | ☐ run | **B** | ☐ has run | **C** | ☐ ran | **D** | ☐ had run |

## Writing

### Part 1

*Here are five sentences about travelling.*
*Complete the second sentence in each pair so that it means the same as the first sentence.*
*You can use one to three words (and no more than three) to fill in the gaps.*
*You mustn't use the same words as in the first sentence.*
*Write only the missing words on the answer sheet. There is an example at the beginning (0).*

0. Soon there will only be one international airport left in Berlin.
   Before long there is ______________________ only one international airport in Berlin.
   *Answer sheet:* 0: going to be

1. My favourite way to travel is always by train.
   I like to travel by train __________________________ any other way.

2. As soon as the taxi is here we can go.
   We can go __________________________ the taxi arrives.

3. My sister has already travelled to London three times this year.
   This year my sister has already __________________________ to London three times.

4. My grandmother doesn't like to go in planes as she's quite afraid of flying.
   Because she's scared to fly my grandmother __________________________ by plane.

5. If you can't afford to fly to Moscow you'll have to take the train.
   __________________________ you have enough money to fly, you'll have to travel to Moscow by train.

### Part 2

*After having taken part in a school exchange with your twin school in England, you write an e-mail (35–45 words) to your pen friend.*

6. In your e-mail you …
   - thank them for the time you spent with their family this summer,
   - mention what you most enjoyed or benefited from during your time in England,
   - say how much you are looking forward to seeing your pen friend in Germany later in the year.

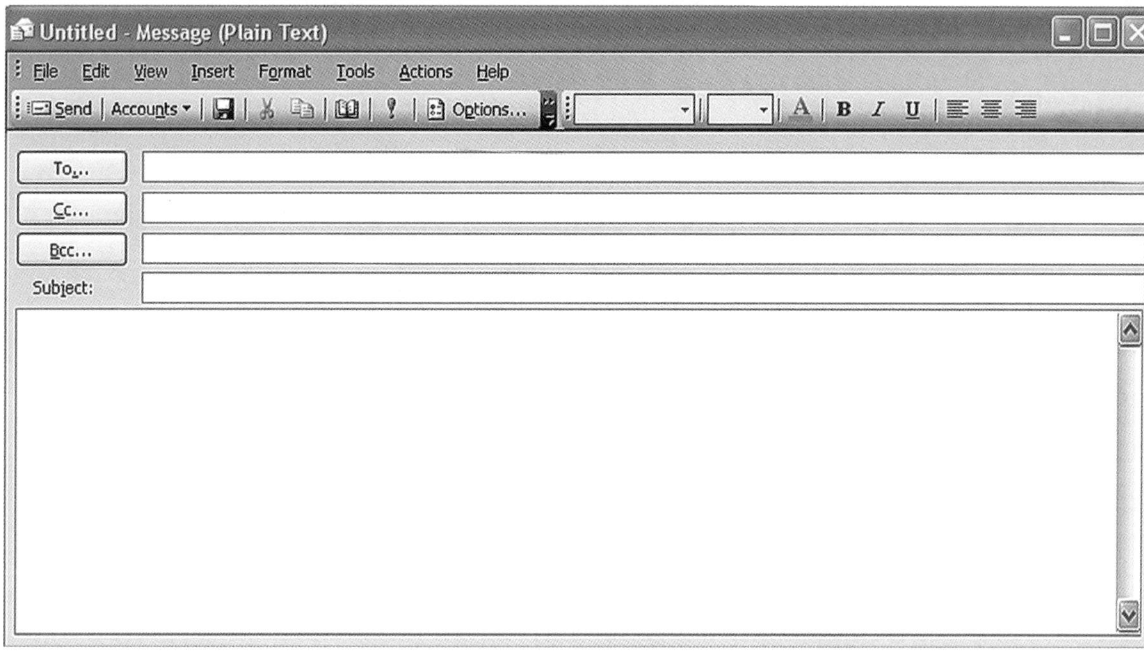


## Part 3

*Choose one of the two tasks 7 or 8 and write about 100 words.*
*Indicate which task you have chosen on your answer sheet.*

7. A friend from an online social networking website writes to you: He or she asks you when the best time would be to visit your hometown, and what you would recommend for visitors. Answer his/her questions.

8. Use the following sentence to start a story.
"He counted the small change in his pockets – it was nowhere near enough."

## Listening

### Part 1

Track 1

*Listen to the texts. Tick (✓) the correct picture.*
*Mark A, B or C on your answer sheet. There is an example at the beginning (0).*

0. Which instrument is the woman going to be learning?

A ☐

B ☑

C ☐

1. What did the woman order in the café?

A ☐

B ☐

C ☐

2. What are the two speakers going to do tonight?

A ☐

B ☐

C ☐

3. How is the family going to travel when they go on holiday?

A ☐

B ☐

C ☐

4. Where does Kate Bush rank in the all-time classics?

A ☐

B ☐

C ☐

5. On which day could the exhibition be open?

A ☐

B ☐

C ☐

6. Who is in hospital at the moment?

A ☐

B ☐

C ☐

## Part 2

Track 2

*You will hear a conversation between the manager of a nursing home and the daughter of a potential resident.*
*Tick (✓) the correct box and mark A, B or C on your answer sheet.*

7. The name of the nursing home is …

**A** ☐ Sylvan Pines.

**B** ☐ Silver Pines.

**C** ☐ Silent Pines.

8. The woman's mother is …
   **A** ☐ sixty-eight years old.
   **B** ☐ eighty-six years old.
   **C** ☐ eighty-five years old.

9. The woman's mother should move into a nursing home because …
   **A** ☐ her daughter can't look after her mother's house because she is at work the whole day.
   **B** ☐ she feels bored at home.
   **C** ☐ she can't move in with her daughter. She would be on her own there most of the time.

10. The library has …
   **A** ☐ nearly twenty thousand books.
   **B** ☐ books, newspapers, magazines and DVDs.
   **C** ☐ nothing to offer for people who are visually impaired.

11. The food provided in the nursing home is …
   **A** ☐ vegetarian.
   **B** ☐ chosen on the advice of medical staff.
   **C** ☐ low-fat and sugar-free.

12. The building being built is …
   **A** ☐ a new swimming pool.
   **B** ☐ a new library.
   **C** ☐ a new sports hall.

## Part 3

Track 3

*You will now hear a radio programme about young people's options after leaving school. Look for the missing information and fill in the gaps.*

**What have you done after leaving school?**

**The new radio programme:** The presenter is talking about a group of students who took their (13) ________________ at Gillingham Comprehensive School ten years ago. The programme will follow the students to find out what they are doing now.

**The people interviewed:** The interviewees have followed different paths. Six of them went on to (14) ______________ at university, where four of them (15) ______________.

**The locations mentioned:** Five of the students involved in the programme went on to live and work (16) ______________, some in the EU, and some in other parts of the world.

**The kind of work that will be discussed:** The people interviewed for the programme are now all working in very different areas. The first two former students who will be interviewed are now working in different environments – one is involved in research in the (17) ______________, and the other is a (18) ______________ consultant in the Gulf state of Dubai.

**The first interviewee:** The first ex-student of Gillingham Comprehensive School who will be interviewed is called (19) ______________. Since 2004 he has worked on a research ship for (20) ______________ of the year. He talks about the jump he had to make from (21) ______________ to practical work – including an encounter with a (22) ______________. He will also talk about what life is like on board a research ship – apparently, it is mostly (23) ____________________ with (24) __________________________.

## Part 4

Track 4

*Read the statements below. Then listen to the conversation between a man and a woman who are talking about the man's recent holiday.*
*Decide if the statements are true or false. Tick (✓) **A** for **true** and **B** for **false**.*

| | A | B |
|---|---|---|
| 25. The woman would be scared to go to Moscow. | ☐ | ☐ |
| 26. The man didn't travel from London to Budapest non-stop. | ☐ | ☐ |
| 27. The man would rather have flown than taken a train. | ☐ | ☐ |
| 28. The man had expected Budapest to be more focused on tourists than it was. | ☐ | ☐ |
| 29. Food in Hungary is as expensive as it is in England. | ☐ | ☐ |
| 30. Being a vegetarian, the woman does not thank the man for having bought her a salami. | ☐ | ☐ |

## Speaking

### Part 1

*In the oral exam there are usually two candidates, an interlocutor and an examiner who observes the conversations. In the first part of the exam the interlocutor asks each candidate about personal details, everyday life, hobbies etc. Here are some possible questions.*

#### Introduction

1. Good morning/afternoon/evening. My name is …
2. What is your name, please?
3. Could you tell me your surname please? And how do you spell that?

#### Questions

4. Could you please tell me where you live?
5. Where do you come from?
6. How many people do you live with?
7. Have you lived here long?
8. Where do you work/study/go to school?
9. Studying: Where do you study? What are you studying?
10. Working: Where do you work? What is your job?
11. School: Which subject do you like best? Do you think English is one of your better subjects? Do you hope to be able to use English in the future, in work or everyday life?
12. Could you please tell us what you like to do in your free time?
13. Do you have any hobbies?
14. Could you please tell us briefly what you did last night/last weekend?
15. Could you please tell us briefly what you did on your last holiday?

### Part 2

*We are going to describe a situation to you both. You'll then both talk to each other to discuss the topic. There are some pictures to give you ideas on the next page.*
*The topic for this section is how English can be used.*
*The situation is: Someone you know is thinking about taking an English course.*
*Can you help him her decide by explaining how English can be useful in your job or everyday life? English can be very useful for certain jobs – which ones can you suggest?*
*Look at the pictures to help you gather ideas, and then talk about this topic together.*

EXIT

Apply Now

www

## Part 3

*Each of you is now going to be given a photograph. Both pictures have to do with reading. I want you both to take a minute to look at your photograph, because you are going to be asked to describe your photographs to each other.*
*Candidate A will start – Candidate B, just listen and then it's your turn.*
*When you're looking at your photographs, think about which words you will need to describe what you see. Think about things like:*

- *What kind of picture is it?*
- *Who is in the picture?*
- *What are they doing?*
- *How does the picture relate to your experience? Is it something you know and / or are familiar with?*

Photo for Candidate A:

Photo for Candidate B:

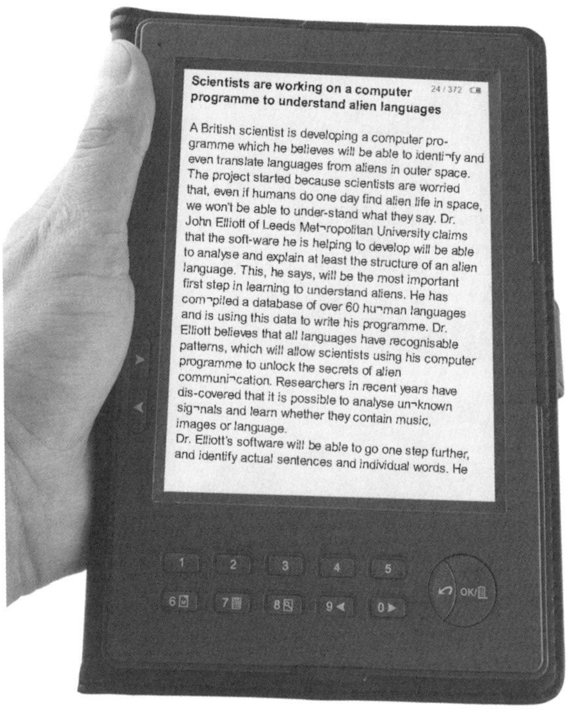


## Part 4

*Your pictures both showed people involved with books and reading in very different situations. Each of you will now use both photographs to talk briefly about books and reading. How have things changed? Is it good that the world of books and reading is changing the way it is? With which of the two pictures do you feel more comfortable?*
*Now discuss.*

# Lösungsvorschläge

## Reading

### Part 1

1. **A** ☐ The restaurant is going to close for the summer because there are no customers.
   **B** ☑ Alfredo's is going to look different when it opens again later in the summer.
   **C** ☐ The restaurant will be closed for over a month while the kitchens are being repaired.

2. **A** ☐ The contents must be poured into water and then brought to the boil for 10 minutes.
   **B** ☑ The contents should be poured into boiling water and then kept on a low heat.
   **C** ☐ Pour salt into boiling water and cook for 10–12 minutes before adding the contents of the bag.

3. **A** ☐ Passengers must bring at least two pieces of luggage with them when they come on board.
   **B** ☐ Passengers must store all their luggage in the space above their seat or under their seat.
   **C** ☑ Travellers can only bring two pieces of hand luggage with them, and these must be carefully stored under the seat in front of them or in the space above their seat.

4. **A** ☐ The bus journey takes twenty minutes and makes three stops.
   **B** ☑ Visitors in wheelchairs will need help when they get to the abbey.
   **C** ☐ The abbey is on the way to the village of Lower Brockhampton.

### Part 2

| 5 | 6 | 7 | 8 | 9 |
|---|---|---|---|---|
| C | – | E | B | D |

### Part 3

| | A | B |
|---|---|---|
| 10. The American scientist Dr. John Elliott has developed a computer programme which will help us understand alien languages. | ☐ | ☑ |
| 11. Over 60 human languages are included in the database which the software uses to analyse signals from outer space. | ☑ | ☐ |
| 12. Scientists are now able to listen to unknown signals and find out if they contain images, musical elements or language. | ☑ | ☐ |

13. The software will be able to translate different types of words. ☐ ☑

14. Dr. Elliott says that the project is very difficult because not all languages follow patterns. ☐ ☑

15. Because aliens are so much more intelligent than humans, there is very little chancc of us being able to understand their languages. ☐ ☑

16. Dr. Elliott's software is designcd to be able to analyse at least the structure of alien languages, even if it won't be able to understand what is being said. ☑ ☐

17. The database of over 60 human languages will be used to try to talk to the aliens, in the hope that they will understand at least some of our human languages. ☐ ☑

18. British scientists don't believe that it is possible that Dr. Elliott's software will ever work. ☐ ☑

19. American scientists are interested in Dr. Elliott's work and are very supportive. ☑ ☐

## Part 4

20. What is the author of the text doing?

**A** ☐ Wishing three 1980s pop stars a happy birthday.
**B** ☐ Explaining why Prince is so strange today.
**C** ☑ Giving a short overview of the development of three 1980s pop stars.
**D** ☐ Giving an objective look at pop music in the 1980s.

21. What do you think the author's attitude is to the pop stars mentioned?

**A** ☑ The author likes Prince more than the others.
**B** ☐ The author thinks that Michael Jackson and Madonna were the greatest pop stars of their time.
**C** ☐ The author thinks that Prince was too weird to be a good pop star.
**D** ☐ The author thinks that the quality of Madonna's music is still the same.

22. Does the author have an opinion about pop stars still making music when they're 50?

**A** ☐ The author thinks it's wrong and that they should stop embarrassing themselves.
**B** ☑ The author doesn't give a clear opinion on the subject.
**C** ☐ The author's opinion is that people can continue making music as long as they like.
**D** ☐ The author's attitude is that some pop stars can still perform when they're 50, but that most of them should stop earlier.

23. What impression of the 1980s do you get from the text?

**A** ☑ The author thinks the 1980s were a very important time for pop music.

**B** ☐ The 1980s were a decade of bad taste and poor music.

**C** ☐ They were a very wild and rebellious time in which teenagers fought against their parents.

**D** ☐ It was boring because there was no Internet.

24. Choose the summary (A, B, C or D) which best applies to the text.

**A** ☑ Being an individual and following your own instincts is a good way to keep the respect of your fans.

**B** ☐ If pop stars carry on making music and performing for too long they become boring; nobody wants to see them anymore.

**C** ☐ Pop music is for children and teenagers. Adults shouldn't be listening to it and they certainly shouldn't be performing it.

**D** ☐ The best way to stay successful and popular is to look at what people want you to do, and then to try to do exactly that.

## Language Elements

| | A | B | C | D |
|---|---|---|---|---|
| 1 | ☑ home | ☐ museum | ☐ filled | ☐ famous |
| 2 | ☐ since | ☑ after | ☐ on | ☐ at |
| 3 | ☐ the police | ☐ she | ☐ a visitor | ☑ guests |
| 4 | ☑ corridors | ☐ cupboards | ☐ beds | ☐ streets |
| 5 | ☐ seen | ☐ feared | ☐ listened | ☑ heard |
| 6 | ☐ researched | ☑ discovered | ☐ figured out | ☐ investigated |
| 7 | ☐ was | ☐ have being | ☐ has been | ☑ have been |
| 8 | ☑ searches | ☐ seeks | ☐ watches | ☐ look |
| 9 | ☐ run | ☐ has run | ☑ ran | ☐ had run |

## Writing

### Part 1

1. I like to travel by train **more than** any other way.
2. We can go **when** the taxi arrives.
3. This year my sister has already **been / flown / gone** to London three times.
4. Because she's scared to fly my grandmother **won't travel / can't travel** by plane.
5. **Unless** you have enough money to fly, you'll have to travel to Moscow by train.

### Part 2

6.

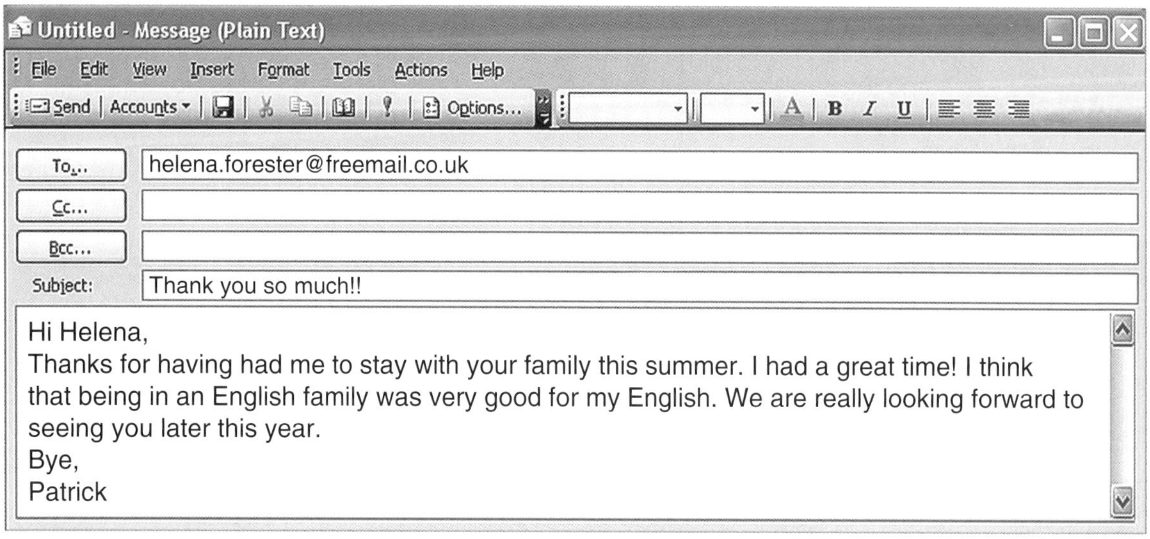

Untitled - Message (Plain Text)

To... helena.forester@freemail.co.uk

Cc...

Bcc...

Subject: Thank you so much!!

Hi Helena,
Thanks for having had me to stay with your family this summer. I had a great time! I think that being in an English family was very good for my English. We are really looking forward to seeing you later this year.
Bye,
Patrick

*(46 words)*

### Part 3

7. The best time to visit our town is probably in the autumn – that's when most of the tourists have left already, and it's before the weather gets too cold and uncomfortable. Spring is also very nice here, but I would definitely say that summer is too busy, and winter is too cold. As far as things to do here are concerned there's a lot to see if you want to do standard tourist things – a lot of historical sights and important buildings. But that's not always so interesting – there are a lot of cool places in the city, new galleries and night clubs. *(103 words)*

8. He counted the small change in his pockets – it was nowhere near enough. The tickets cost more than £3 each. This was bad because his girlfriend was standing next to him and he had invited her to the cinema tonight. Of course she thought he could pay for the tickets. He felt very embarrassed and wondered where he could get more money quickly. If he went to the bank to get more money, they would be late for the film. If he asked his girlfriend, she would think he was a loser. He thought it might be a good idea to say he felt sick and they just went home. *(111 words)*

## Listening: Tapescript

Track 1

### Part 1

0. MAN: So have you decided what you want to do?
   WOMAN: My brother plays guitar really well, I thought I might try the drums so that we could play together.
   MAN: Oh! I don't like that idea. Tell you what, I'll pay for piano lessons, how's that? Drums are too noisy for me.
   WOMAN: OK, why not? Playing drums is too much like hard work anyway.

1. MAN: Good morning, what can I get for you?
   WOMAN: Morning, I'd like a cappuccino to go please.
   MAN: Would you like anything else? The muffins are on special offer.
   WOMAN: No, thank you, just a cappuccino.
   MAN: That'll be £1.50, please. Have a nice day!

2. MAN: What time will you be finished?
   WOMAN: I'll be out of the office by six thirty. What do you want to do tonight?
   MAN: The new Korean restaurant near my house is supposed to be great.
   WOMAN: But I wanted to see the new Russell Crowe film. The restaurant will still be there next week, won't it?
   MAN: Ha ha ha, yes it will. I'll get the tickets then and I'll pick you up outside the art gallery near your office at six thirty.

3. WOMAN: The kids would love to fly, you know.
   MAN: Yes, I know, but it's very expensive. How about a bike ride?
   WOMAN: From Southampton to Edinburgh? No thank you. That would take a week.
   MAN: OK, OK, you're right. I'll have a look at the train timetable then.
   WOMAN: Remember to reserve seats, it'll be full at the weekend.

4. Here are the all-time classic charts for this week, as voted for by you, our listeners: number five is Oasis. Coldplay come in at number four. The third place goes to those other kings of Britpop, Blur. And the top two … Second place goes to Kate Bush, and number one: your top act, this week at least, is that Birmingham institution, the godfathers of heavy metal, Black Sabbath!

5. MAN: You have a wonderful collection here. I'm looking forward to seeing the exhibition.
   WOMAN: Yes, it should be very good when we get all the pictures in one room; but I won't be able to organise it for a few weeks. It'll be autumn before the exhibition is ready.

6. WOMAN: I'm afraid we had some bad news today, dear.
   MAN: Oh no, what's happened? Is something wrong with my sister's baby?
   WOMAN: No, Susan and little Emily are OK. It's your mother. Your dad just called, she's in hospital. She hurt her leg when she fell in the kitchen.

Track 2

## Part 2

MAN: Welcome to the Sylvan Pines Nursing Home. I understand you're interested in our services and facilities?

WOMAN: Yes, I am. My mother is finding it difficult to live alone, and her house is too big for her to look after. I can't have her living with me because I work until late in the evening all week.

MAN: I understand. How old is your mother?

WOMAN: She'll be 86 this summer. She's very nervous about the idea of moving into a nursing home.

MAN: Of course, I fully understand. Well, if you'll follow me, I can take you on a brief tour and point out some of our features and services. This is the lounge, of course, our residents can play games, watch television, take part in discussion clubs or just relax in company in this area. Down the hall here we have the library; apart from over thirty thousand books, we also offer a selection of daily newspapers and a variety of magazines, and our media library is also growing. We have a wide selection of films and television programmes on DVD as well as an extensive collection of books on tape or CD. Through the window here you can see our sports area. Our residents can enjoy table tennis and badminton in good weather. The kitchens are to the right; here's a copy of our menu plan for this week so that you can get an idea of what's on offer. We can provide meals for specific needs, vegetarian of course, as well as sugar-free or other diets. All the menus are put together with medical staff to make sure that the best balance between good food and healthy eating is maintained. Here at Sylvan Pines we like our residents to be happy and healthy. Over there you can see the building site; that's where our new swimming pool is being built. We will have three pools for different needs, with full disabled access and a special staff trained in lifeguard duties and water-based physiotherapy. We also plan to build a new sports hall in the near future. Now if you'd like to follow me to my office, I can show you some more detailed information on our services and the monthly costs.

Track 3

## Part 3

The first in our new series on what to do after leaving school will focus on a group of students from Gillingham Comprehensive School. The class took their A-levels a decade ago, and the eight former students we have interviewed for our programme have all followed very different paths since leaving school. Six of the eight students went on to university, where four of them finished, gaining degrees in subjects ranging from Geology to Biochemistry to Medieval Linguistics. Of the eight we talked to, five have left the UK to live and work abroad, and here again we are looking at a wide variety – two moved to countries in the European union, one to the US, one to Dubai, and one is now working on a scientific research ship in the Antarctic. The two students who did not go on to study, and the two who dropped out before they finished, have also been followed up by our reporters. The two non-students are both working in low-income jobs in their home town; and of the two dropouts, one is currently on tour with a rock band in eastern Europe, while the other is now working as a chauffeur for the owner of one of London's most infamous night clubs. We wanted to know from the students, who had agreed back then to allow us to follow up on their progress ten years later, how they felt about the path they had followed up to now, and whether or not they regretted their choice of studies, or their choice not to study. Our first programme will be about Tim, now working in sub-zero temperatures in a floating tin can somewhere in the Antarctic seas, and Rebecca, who works as a financial consultant to a sheikh in the rapidly-growing multi-billion dollar property development industry in Dubai. Tim finished his studies in Marine Biology at Cambridge University in 2004, and has been working eight-month shifts on the research ship *Pinafore* ever since. It's been difficult to get hold of him at times, but our reporter caught up with him while he was on leave in the UK earlier this month. Tim had a lot to tell us about the jump from theory in the laboratory to nearly getting his hand bitten off by a walrus. And he'll also be telling us how his years at university taught him how to deal with long evenings with nothing to do. Rebecca on the other hand was kind enough to let our reporter get a glimpse into the luxurious lifestyles of one of the most wealthy places on Earth. She will be talking to us about why she thinks her time at university did nothing to prepare her for her life now, as well as about why racism will never be completely defeated, and what it's like to work as an unmarried European woman in a traditionally male society which is trying to change with the times. Next week our programme will be back in England to talk to Steve and Trevor, both working as shelf stockers at the new Lidl discount supermarket in the small town of Hindon. So stay with us and listen to Tim and Rebecca after the break …

## Part 4

Track 4

WOMAN: So how was your holiday? You wanted to fly to Moscow, didn't you?

MAN: Originally, yes. That was the plan.

WOMAN: Ah, I see. I guess that didn't work out, then?

MAN: No, unfortunately not. Lots of people told me that Russia is not safe for British citizens – I don't know whether that's true or not, it sounds a bit paranoid, but I decided not to risk it.

WOMAN: And? So where did you go then?

MAN: Budapest, Hungary. I took the train through the Chunnel to Germany, stayed for a couple of nights with an old friend of mine in Berlin, and then took the train to Budapest.

WOMAN: Wow. That must have been really tiring.

MAN: It was OK. The train journey from Berlin to Kileti in Budapest is 12 hours. That's an awfully long time to spend in a train, but on the other hand it's more comfortable than flying, right?

WOMAN: I guess. At least you can move around on a train. But 12 hours – that's half a day, just gone on travelling!

MAN: It wasn't so bad, really. We went through some beautiful landscapes in Germany, and Slovakia was a bit dull, but as soon as you enter Hungary the countryside is just amazing.

WOMAN: You haven't been to Hungary before, have you?

MAN: No, this was my first time. It was odd, Budapest has got such a beautiful centre, and there are a lot of tourists, but it seems to be kind of unspoiled in a way. It was a lot less of a tourist trap than I expected it to be.

WOMAN: Must be really cheap too, I guess?

MAN: Surprisingly, no. Beer and taxis are cheap, but everything else is pretty much European standard – well, not UK standard, prices here are just offensive, food and clothes and stuff is just as dear as it is in Germany or France. But I had money, I knew that Moscow would have been very expensive, so I'd saved up quite a bit. I did buy myself some nice boots and a winter coat – and look, I even got something for you.

WOMAN: Oh! A salami. Uh … thanks. I guess you forgot I'm vegetarian, right?

## Listening: Solutions

### Part 1

1. What did the woman order in the café?

A ☑ B ☐ C ☐

2. What are the two speakers going to do tonight?

A ☐ B ☐ C ☑

3. How is the family going to travel when they go on holiday?

A ☐ B ☐ C ☑

4. Where does Kate Bush rank in the all-time classics?

A ☐ B ☑ C ☐

5. On which day could the exhibition be open?

A ☑

B ☐

C ☐

6. Who is in hospital at the moment?

A ☑

B ☐

C ☐

## Part 2

7. The name of the nursing home is …
   - **A** ☑ Sylvan Pines.
   - **B** ☐ Silver Pines.
   - **C** ☐ Silent Pines.

8. The woman's mother is …
   - **A** ☐ sixty-eight years old.
   - **B** ☐ eighty-six years old.
   - **C** ☑ eighty-five years old.

9. The woman's mother should move into a nursing home because …
   - **A** ☐ her daughter can't look after her mother's house because she is at work the whole day.
   - **B** ☐ she feels bored at home.
   - **C** ☑ she can't move in with her daughter. She would be on her own there most of the time.

10. The library has …
   - **A** ☐ nearly twenty thousand books.
   - **B** ☑ books, newspapers, magazines and DVDs.
   - **C** ☐ nothing to offer for people who are visually impaired.

11. The food provided in the nursing home is …
   - **A** ☐ vegetarian.
   - **B** ☑ chosen on the advice of medical staff.
   - **C** ☐ low-fat and sugar-free.

12. The building being built is …
   - **A** ☑ a new swimming pool.
   - **B** ☐ a new library.
   - **C** ☐ a new sports hall.

## Part 3

**What have you done after leaving school?**

**The new radio programme:** The presenter is talking about a group of students who took their (13) *A-levels* at Gillingham Comprehensive School ten years ago. The programme will follow the students to find out what they are doing now.

**The people interviewed:** The interviewees have followed different paths. Six of them went on to (14) *study* at university, where four of them (15) *graduated / finished their studies*.

**The locations mentioned:** Five of the students involved in the programme went on to live and work (16) *abroad*, some in the EU, and some in other parts of the world.

**The kind of work that will be discussed:** The people interviewed for the programme are now all working in very different areas. The first two former students who will be interviewed are now working in different environments – one is involved in research in the (17) *Antarctic*, and the other is a (18) *financial* consultant in the Gulf state of Dubai.

**The first interviewee:** The first ex-student of Gillingham Comprehensive School who will be interviewed is called (19) *Tim*. Since 2004 he has worked on a research ship for (20) *eight months* of the year. He talks about the jump he had to make from (21) *theory* to practical work – including an encounter with a (22) *walrus*. He will also talk about what life is like on board a research ship – apparently, it is mostly (23) *long evenings* with (24) *nothing to do*.

### Part 4

| | | A | B |
|---|---|---|---|
| 25. | The woman would be scared to go to Moscow. | ☐ | ☑ |
| 26. | The man didn't travel from London to Budapest non-stop. | ☑ | ☐ |
| 27. | The man would rather have flown than taken a train. | ☐ | ☑ |
| 28. | The man had expected Budapest to be more focused on tourists than it was. | ☑ | ☐ |
| 29. | Food in Hungary is as expensive as it is in England. | ☐ | ☑ |
| 30. | Being a vegetarian, the woman does not thank the man for having bought her a salami. | ☐ | ☑ |

## Speaking

### Part 1

**Introduction**

1. Good morning, it's nice to meet you.
2. My name is …
3. Yes, of course. My surname is … It's spelled …

**Questions**

4. I live in … / My house is in … / I live with my family in …
5. I was born in … / I originally come from … / I come from around here … / I was born here …
6. I live with … people / There are … people in my family / I live with my parents, my sister, and my two brothers.
7. I've always lived here. / We only moved here recently. / I've lived here since … / I've lived here for … years/months.
8. I work / study / go to school here in the area. / My workplace / school is in …
9. I study at … college / university.
   I'm studying … / I study …
10. I work at … *[name of company]* / I work in … *[name of area, e.g. retail, office work, engineering]*
    My job is … / I work as a … / My job involves … *[briefly describe the activities your job involves]*
11. The subject I like best is … / … is my favourite subject.
    Yes, I think it is. / I like to think so, yes. / Yes, I feel confident in English. / I know I can always improve my English, but it is one of my better subjects, yes.

Yes, I hope I can. / Yes, I would love to have the opportunity to use English in my work later in life.

12. In my free time, I like to ... / I usually do ... in my free time. / I like to ... in my free time.
13. Yes, I have a few hobbies. They include ... / My hobbies are ...
14. Last night? I went to the cinema with some friends. / Last weekend, I went on a trip to the mountains / the sea.
15. On my last holiday I went to ... and did ... / My last holiday was great, I went to ... / The last holiday I had I spent in ..., where I did ...

## Part 2

CANDIDATE A: Looking at these pictures, I think that they show many ways in which English would be useful. A friend of mine is thinking about taking an English course, too.

CANDIDATE B: That's certainly a good idea. English is very important when you travel to other countries, because it's a language that is spoken almost everywhere.

CANDIDATE A: That's true. English is also very important when you want to research things for your work or just for yourself – especially if you want to learn things from international media.

CANDIDATE B: Yes, because not everything on the Internet is going to be in your own language.

CANDIDATE A: Communication over the Internet, for private things like chat rooms or e-mails, and also for official business like booking flights or learning more about a place you want to visit, is also easier in English.

CANDIDATE B: It's very important to be able to speak English if you're applying for jobs, too – lots of employees expect the people who work for them to be able to speak English – even if it doesn't actually happen much in the job ...

## Part 3

CANDIDATE A: It is a very old-fashioned painting of a man in a library. He is standing on a ladder and looking at a book. Everything looks very dusty and crowded, and the shelves are full of books. The man is reading, or looking for something, and obviously has to climb up a ladder and really search to find what he wants. I've never used such a library myself. The one I go to in my hometown is much more modern. You can use the computer to search for the book you need and then you know in which section of the library you'll find it. The picture makes me think of a museum or old films.

CANDIDATE B: My picture is very, very modern: it is a photograph of an e-book. You don't actually see the person who is using the e-book, you just see the person's hands. Reading an e-book is very different from reading a "normal" book. Whoever is reading the e-book doesn't have to do much at all to read what he or she wants. The book you want to read is in the computer and you just have to use the buttons to "turn the pages" or look for the text you need. No physical action is necessary to search for something. I have never used an e-book myself but I would like to try it sometime.

## Part 4

The two pictures show very different ways of reading, and different ways of storing and getting access to literature or texts. The first one is an extreme example but it is more familiar to me because even today, we still need books. Maybe in the future there won't be any printed books at all anymore, and everything will be in e-books or on the Internet – but at the moment we still need and read books. I think that books which are printed on paper are better than words on a computer screen, because they are more individual. Books always feel different, look different, and even smell different. The way people store information changes all the time, from paintings on cave walls to writing on animal skins and then to printing, and now that we have the ability to keep all this information and all these stories in digital form, books will probably just vanish at some point. That will be a sad thing, in my opinion, but it is of course cheaper and easier to use digital information than to print out thousands of copies of a book.

## Reading

### Part 1

*Read the texts and choose the correct explanation.*
*Tick (✓) the correct sentences and mark the letter (A–C) on your answer sheet.*
*There is an example at the beginning (0).*

0.

- ☐ **A** No entry!
- ☐ **B** Only people in authority may go beyond this point.
- ☑ **C** Only people with permission may enter.

1.

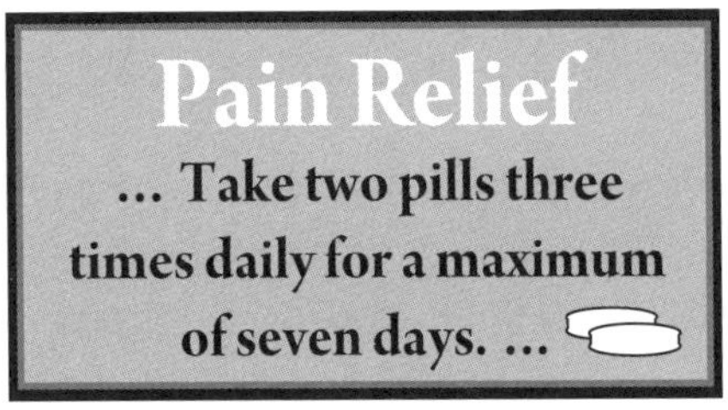


- ☐ **A** Three pills every two days for a week.
- ☐ **B** Six pills a day for a week.
- ☐ **C** Two pills every three days for a week.

2.

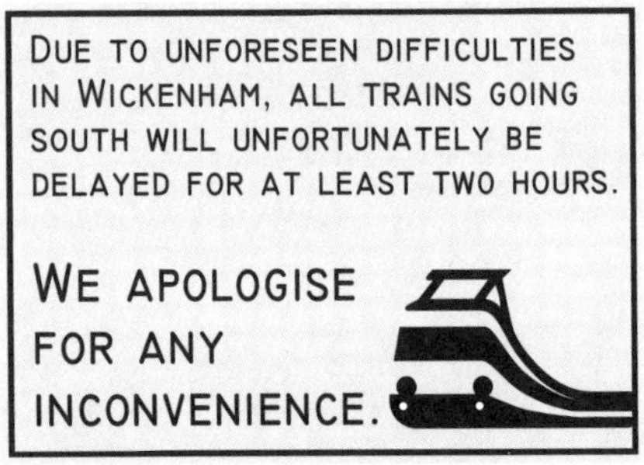


- ☐ **A** Technical problems in a northern station mean that trains will be delayed.
- ☐ **B** A planned strike will delay all southbound trains.
- ☐ **C** Passengers at Wickenham have to wait two hours for their trains.

3.

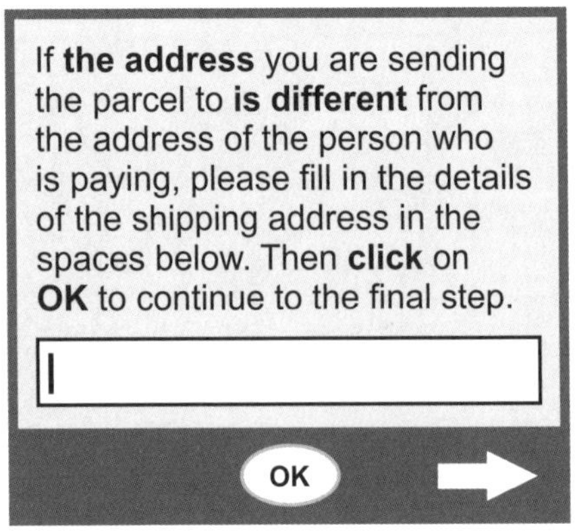


- ☐ **A** If you want the items sent to a different address from the one from which you are paying, then enter the address you want the parcel sent to below.
- ☐ **B** If you want the items to be sent to the person paying for them, then write their address here.
- ☐ **C** If you want someone else to pay for the items, then write their address in the space below.

4. 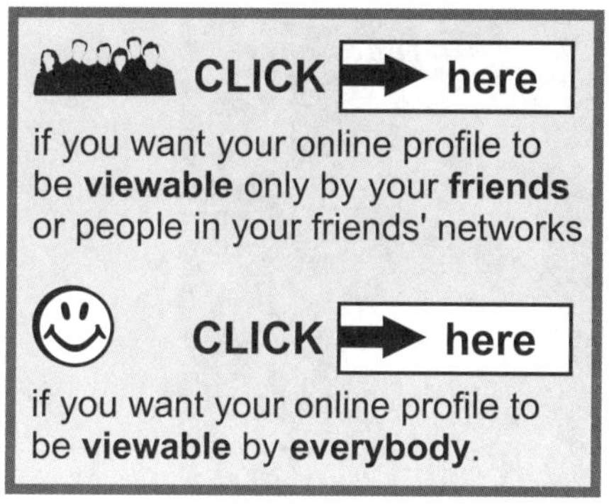


- ☐ **A** Here you can decide which of your friends can view your profile.
- ☐ **B** Here you can decide who you want to be friends with.
- ☐ **C** Here you can decide who you want to be able to view your profile.

## Part 2

*You are taking a walk through the city of Galway.*
*Match the signs (A–H) with the correct explanation (5–9).*
*Mark the correct letter on your answer sheet.*

5. You have to clean up after your dog here.
6. In this café you have to order at the counter.
7. In this café you can write e-mails.
8. Your dog isn't allowed to run free here.
9. In this café you can order at your table.

**A**

**B**

**C**

**D**

E

F

G

H

| 5 | 6 | 7 | 8 | 9 |
|---|---|---|---|---|
| | | | | |

## Part 3

*After reading the text, decide if the statements are true or false.*
*Tick (✓)* ***A*** *for* ***true*** *and* ***B*** *for* ***false****.*
*Mark the correct letter on your answer sheet.*

| | A | B |
|---|---|---|
| 10. The most recent victim was a young man. | ☐ | ☐ |
| 11. The MP is concerned about so-called "memory walls" on some online community sites. | ☐ | ☐ |
| 12. Young people who participate in online communities are always aware of the consequences of their actions in the "real world". | ☐ | ☐ |
| 13. The suicide victims all knew each other. | ☐ | ☐ |
| 14. There were 13 suicides during the past year. | ☐ | ☐ |
| 15. Police think that the victims were members of a "cult". | ☐ | ☐ |
| 16. The mother of one of the boys tried to talk to her son about the deaths of his friends. | ☐ | ☐ |
| 17. Young people are advised not to talk about the suicides. | ☐ | ☐ |

18. The spokesperson for an online community website said that they work together with various groups to provide a safe environment for their users. ☐ ☐
19. The article is about fears that online communities may encourage young people to attempt suicide. ☐ ☐

**Web worries after suicide series**

Social networking websites could be "romanticising" suicide, a British MP claims after a series of suicides among young people from her area in the past year.

The most recent victim was found hanged at her home, and a girl who is believed to know her attempted suicide a day later. The MP will raise Internet use issues with a local focus group, which includes the police and members of the local health trust, schools and council. She is growing increasingly worried by the appearance of so-called "memory walls" on networking sites, where members leave messages to mark the death of a friend. "The worrying part about Internet sites is, it isn't a real world," she said. "The things that happen there don't necessarily demonstrate the consequences. I'm particularly concerned about this false romanticism of the memory wall that seems to give some sort of romantic idea of suicide without conveying the tragedy and wasted lives," she said. Police investigating the latest incidents are trying to discover whether the girls had made contact on the Internet. But police think that while some of the seven young people knew each other, there was nothing to link them all. Last summer, locals were "desperately concerned" about the number of suicides among young men in the area. The number of suicides among people under 26 in the area in the past year was 13. Some newspapers have compared the series of suicides to a "cult". One of the suicides hanged himself in February 2007. He had been friends with two boys who had been found dead weeks earlier. The boy's mother said she had talked to her son about the deaths of his friends: "He was quite upset because he went to school with them. I said to him: 'You would never do that to me, would you?' He said 'I'd never do that to you – I wouldn't hurt you.' I think it was a couple of days later that he did it." Parents say that the children should talk to somebody, even if it's a stranger, about suicides among their age group. A spokesperson for a social networking site said: "The loss of any young life is always distressing. We will work closely with the authorities to provide any assistance which will help them with their investigations. We have close relationships with law enforcement agencies and public safety partners to provide support and advice for our users. We are committed to providing our members with the safest possible environment online."

## Part 4

*After reading the text, answer the questions below.*
*For each question, mark the correct letter (A–D) on your answer sheet.*

**Children would rather read gossip magazines than books**

British children are reading celebrity gossip magazines instead of books, especially if the novels are longer than 100 pages, a recent study shows. Boys and girls as young as 11 said they preferred absorbing the exploits of pop stars and models such as Amy Winehouse and Kate Moss to reading books by Jacqueline Wilson or Philip Pullman. But isn't it clear that children who choose to read gossip magazines – most of which are aimed at an adult audience – and surf the Internet instead of reading books will damage their development? Some people argue that children should be encouraged to read whatever they like – as long as they are reading. The study found that Shakespeare was very unpopular among the children questioned, as were "books I am made to read by my teachers". Instead, they preferred to read song lyrics on the Internet, their own online blogs, and occasionally film scripts. Four out of the top 10 choices for reading were online texts. It must surely make sense that reading books helps to develop a child's brain. Research shows that one of the best indicators of future academic success is how much children are reading by the age of 16 – the trouble with reading magazines and reading online texts is that you don't get the narrative thread of a story in the same way. When you read a book you are building up the stamina to absorb words for a longer period of time – which of course doesn't happen when you're reading chunks of a magazine or chunks of text on a screen. This unique level of interaction in your head is what is special about reading a book. The survey was of 1,340 children aged between 11 and 14, who were asked to list their 10 favourite and 10 least favourite things to read. Homework was – obviously enough – the most unpopular subject matter, followed by Shakespeare, encyclopaedias, and dictionaries. The survey revealed that 45 per cent of the young people had been told off by adults for not reading proper books. Some people say that we should all appreciate that many young people read "creatively". They say that teenagers today are challenging the traditional definition of reading as being all about books. Some people even claim that it's "wonderful" that 80 per cent of all British teenagers write "creative" online blogs and read other teenagers' blogs and comments. And some people even think that it's good for teenagers to get so involved in "adult" areas – like celebrity gossip stories.

20. The author thinks …

**A** ☐ it's great that children are reading celebrity magazines.

**B** ☐ writing blogs is the best thing teenagers can do with their creativity.

**C** ☐ children should be reading more books.

**D** ☐ reading gossip magazines helps prepare children for today's world.

21. Some people argue that …

**A** ☐ it doesn't matter what children read, as long as they're reading.

**B** ☐ teenagers should only read online to help prepare them for the modern world.

**C** ☐ parents should make sure their children do not only read online.

**D** ☐ reading is all about books.

22. The author's attitude to reading can be described thus:

**A** ☐ Reading books is a unique process and should be encouraged.

**B** ☐ Reading is a rather old-fashioned way to pass on information.

**C** ☐ Reading is important, but it's more important for teenagers to participate in online life.

**D** ☐ Reading is the best way for young people to get involved in adult life.

23. The general attitude among young people as discovered by the survey seems to be that …

**A** ☐ reading is boring and useless.

**B** ☐ homework and school texts like Shakespeare's plays are very unpopular.

**C** ☐ the only books children read are fantasy novels.

**D** ☐ adults always complain too much about what children and teenagers read.

24. Choose the summary below which best applies to the text.

**A** ☐ The text is about the kind of books children have to read and about how much they dislike having to read these particular books.

**B** ☐ The author describes the findings of a recent survey about the reading habits of children and teenagers, and talks briefly about different attitudes to reading.

**C** ☐ The author writes about the reading habits in schools and how parents try to support their children's reading.

**D** ☐ The text is about the psychological processes involved in reading, and how these processes differ between children and adults.

## Part 5

*Read the text. The gaps can be filled in using the words in the lists below.*
*For each space (25–33), mark the correct letter (A–D) on your answer sheet.*
*There is an example at the beginning (0).*

**Technologically challenged**

We bought an external hard (0) _______ for our computer last week. It wasn't something we actually *needed*, that's true, but we had (25) _______ given a DVD-ROM with holiday movies (26) _______ a friend had made in Spain this summer, and he wanted us to watch them. But because we don't want to watch films on our computer screen, we wanted to (27) _______ the computer to the television and watch properly, on a big screen. There were a few problems with this, however … The first problem was that the files on the DVD-ROM were all in odd formats which we couldn't (28) _______. A bad start! A few hours later, we had been told by a friend which programme we needed to open the files. The next problem was already on the way – how do we attach the computer to the television? The cables we had were all wrong. So, off to the shops, buy some cables, come back – next problem; none of the cables (29) _______! So we took our digital camera, took some photos of the places in the computer and the television where we (30) _______ the cables had to go, and went back to the shop to show the nice man the photos. When he had finished laughing (31) _______ us he told us that both our computer and our television were too old – there was no way we could watch films from our computer on our television. Any helpful advice? Only the obvious, of course – it's time to (32) _______ the 21st century. In order to watch someone else's holiday films on DVD, we have to buy a new computer and a new television. (33) _______ it's time to turn off the technology and go and read a book instead?

| | | | | | | | | |
|---|---|---|---|---|---|---|---|---|
| 0 | **A** ☐ | driver | **B** ☑ | drive | **C** ☐ | drives | **D** ☐ | driven |
| 25 | **A** ☐ | been | **B** ☐ | be | **C** ☐ | were | **D** ☐ | being |
| 26 | **A** ☐ | witch | **B** ☐ | what | **C** ☐ | which | **D** ☐ | whose |
| 27 | **A** ☐ | attach | **B** ☐ | attack | **C** ☐ | build | **D** ☐ | hyperlink |
| 28 | **A** ☐ | view | **B** ☐ | understand | **C** ☐ | open | **D** ☐ | copy |
| 29 | **A** ☐ | fit | **B** ☐ | is fitting | **C** ☐ | fits | **D** ☐ | had fit |

| | | | | | | | | | | | |
|---|---|---|---|---|---|---|---|---|---|---|---|
| 30 | **A** | ☐ | think | **B** | ☐ thinking | | **C** | ☐ thoughts | | **D** | ☐ thought |
| 31 | **A** | ☐ | at | **B** | ☐ on | | **C** | ☐ to | | **D** | ☐ for |
| 32 | **A** | ☐ | entering | **B** | ☐ entered | | **C** | ☐ enter | | **D** | ☐ entrance |
| 33 | **A** | ☐ | probably | **B** | ☐ maybe | | **C** | ☐ likely | | **D** | ☐ impossibly |

## Writing

### Part 1

*Here are five sentences about homes and furniture.*
*Complete the second sentence in each pair so that it means the same as the first sentence.*
*You can use one to three words (and no more than three) to fill in the gaps.*
*There is an example at the beginning (0).*

0. I don't have enough space on my desk, I need to get a new one!
My desk is ________________, it's time I got a new one.
*Answer sheet:* 0: too small *or:* not big enough

1. There aren't enough bedrooms in our house for all the guests we're expecting at the weekend.
There are ________________________ people coming this weekend, we don't have space for all of them.

2. It's not fair, my sister's room is much bigger than mine!
My room ________________________ than my sister's!

3. Our kitchen is right behind the dining room.
The dining room is ________________________ the kitchen.

4. We have two big armchairs and a huge sofa in the living room.
There is ________________________ of armchairs and a sofa in the living room.

5. The bookshelves in the living room are between the door to the hall and the door to the kitchen.
There are doors ________________________ of the bookshelves in the living room.

## Part 2

*A friend of yours hurt himself this morning while riding his bike to school and you have gone to the hospital with him.*

6. Write a short text message (35–45 words) to your parents explaining where you are – and why you aren't at school.

## Part 3

*Choose one of the two tasks 7 or 8 below and write a 100-word text.*
*Indicate which task you have chosen on your answer sheet.*

7. The editor of the school magazine has asked you to write a short review of the last concert you went to or the last film you saw in the cinema.

8. Describe what you want to do once you've finished school in a blog entry.

## Listening

### Part 1

Track 5

*Listen to the short texts. Tick (✓) the correct picture.*
*There is an example at the beginning (0).*

0. What does the woman buy?

**A** ☐

**B** ☑

**C** ☐

1. The man is at the airport shortly before the departure. What could be his flight?

**A** ☐

**B** ☐

**C** ☐

2. Why is the train delayed?

**A** ☐

**B** ☐

**C** ☐

3. How much money will the woman get in euros once she's exchanged the pounds for euros?

**A** ☐

**B** ☐

**C** ☐

4. What does the man think the woman should pack?

A ☐

B ☐

C ☐

5. What kind of service does the taxi company offer?

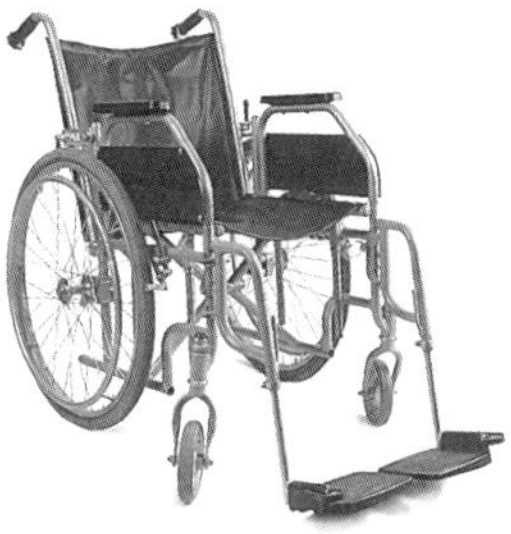
A ☐

B ☐

C ☐

6. What luggage is the passenger taking on board with him?

A ☐

B ☐

C ☐

Track 6

## Part 2

*You will now hear someone call a youth hostel.*
*Tick (✓) the correct box and mark A, B or C on your answer sheet.*

7. The name of the youth hostel is Lulworth …

**A** ☐ Cove.

**B** ☐ Cave.

**C** ☐ Grove.

8. How long does the caller want to stay at the hostel?

**A** ☐ 21/06 to 04/07
**B** ☐ 14/06 to 21/06
**C** ☐ 04/06 to 21/06

9. How many rooms will the caller be booking?

**A** ☐ Two family rooms
**B** ☐ One family room and two singles
**C** ☐ Two single rooms

10. How much do children under 18 have to pay?

**A** ☐ £ 14
**B** ☐ £ 18.95
**C** ☐ £ 10.95

11. Breakfast is …

**A** ☐ not available.
**B** ☐ available, but it costs extra.
**C** ☐ included in the price of the rooms.

12. The caller gives his …

**A** ☐ mobile phone number and e-mail address.
**B** ☐ postal address and telephone number.
**C** ☐ mobile phone number and office number.

Track 7

## Part 3

*Someone is talking about his hometown in England, Christchurch.*
*Look for the missing information and fill in the gaps.*

**Christchurch, UK**

Located: (13) ______________ coast of England

Activities: (14) ______________________ in High Street: events (theatre, concerts) all year round

Sports: (15) ________________________, (16) ___________________ and other water sports.

Museums: (17) _____________________ and (18) ___________________

## Part 4

Track 8

*Read the statements below, then listen to the radio show about learning methods. Decide if the statements are true or false. Tick (✓) **A** for **true** and **B** for **false**. Mark the correct letter on your answer sheet.*

| | A | B |
|---|---|---|
| 19. The studio guest has already finished school. | ☐ | ☐ |
| 20. It's important not to get in a panic about revising for exams. | ☐ | ☐ |
| 21. It helps to make a timetable of the subjects you have to study. | ☐ | ☐ |
| 22. Each study block should be at least two hours long to make sure you learn enough. | ☐ | ☐ |
| 23. If you study foreign languages, it is a good idea to listen to podcasts in this language. | ☐ | ☐ |
| 24. You won't have much time during the exams, so work as fast as possible. | ☐ | ☐ |

# Speaking

## Part 1

*In the oral exam there are usually two candidates, an interlocutor and an examiner who observes the conversations. In the first part of the exam you have to talk to your partner and find out as much as possible about him or her. Use the following ideas, but try to have a natural conversation. Ask only about details you do not already know.*
*You can for example ask your partner about the following aspects:*

- *his/her name*
- *where he/she is from, where he/she lives (details about the house/flat)*
- *how long he/she has been living there, if he/she likes living there*
- *his/her family*
- *if he/she has ever been abroad*
- *his/her likes and dislikes*

## Part 2

*We are going to describe a situation to you both. You'll then talk to each other to discuss the topic. The topic for this section is: Going abroad.*
*The situation is: Candidate B is thinking about taking a summer job in an English-speaking country. Try to find out together which country would be best for candidate B.*
*Look at the pictures for a few minutes to gather ideas; then talk about this topic together.*

## Part 3

*Each of you is now going to be given a photograph. Both pictures are of world leaders. Look at the photograph and then describe your photographs to each other.*
*Candidate A will start – Candidate B, just listen and then it's your turn.*
*Afterwards, please discuss this topic together.*
*When you're looking at your photographs, think about which words you will need to describe what you see. Think about the kind of language you will need. Think about things like:*

- *Who is in the picture? What does his body language tell you?*
- *Which countries do they lead? (If you are not sure, just guess and explain your choice)*
- *What do you know about these countries? What is your opinion of these leaders?*

Candidate A:

Candidate B:

## Part 4

*You and your partner are planning to spend time together next weekend.*
*Discuss*

- *what you could do,*
- *when and where you meet,*
- *how to get there,*
- *how and when to get home.*

*Present your ideas to each other and then try to find a compromise.*

# Lösungsvorschläge

## Reading

### Part 1

1. **A** ☐ Three pills every two days for a week.
   **B** ☑ Six pills a day for a week.
   **C** ☐ Two pills every three days for a week.

2. **A** ☐ Technical problems in a northern station mean that trains will be delayed.
   **B** ☐ A planned strike will delay all southbound trains.
   **C** ☑ Passengers at Wickenham have to wait two hours for their trains.

3. **A** ☑ If you want the items sent to a different address from the one from which you are paying, then enter the address you want the parcel sent to below.
   **B** ☐ If you want the items to be sent to the person paying for them, then write their address here.
   **C** ☐ If you want someone else to pay for the items, then write their address in the space below.

4. **A** ☐ Here you can decide which of your friends can view your profile.
   **B** ☐ Here you can decide who you want to be friends with.
   **C** ☑ Here you can decide who you want to be able to view your profile.

### Part 2

| 5 | 6 | 7 | 8 | 9 |
|---|---|---|---|---|
| D | A | F | H | G |

### Part 3

| | A | B |
|---|---|---|
| 10. The most recent victim was a young man. | ☐ | ☑ |
| 11. The MP is concerned about so-called "memory walls" on some online community sites. | ☑ | ☐ |
| 12. Young people who participate in online communities are always aware of the consequences of their actions in the "real world". | ☐ | ☑ |
| 13. The suicide victims all knew each other. | ☐ | ☑ |

| | | |
|---|---|---|
| 14. There were 13 suicides during the past year. | ☑ | ☐ |
| 15. Police think that the victims were members of a "cult". | ☐ | ☑ |
| 16. The mother of one of the boys tried to talk to her son about the deaths of his friends. | ☑ | ☐ |
| 17. Young people are advised not to talk about the suicides. | ☐ | ☑ |
| 18. The spokesperson for an online community website said that they work together with various groups to provide a safe environment for their users. | ☑ | ☐ |
| 19. The article is about fears that online communities may encourage young people to attempt suicide. | ☑ | ☐ |

**Part 4**

20. The author thinks …

**A** ☐ it's great that children are reading celebrity magazines.
**B** ☐ writing blogs is the best thing teenagers can do with their creativity.
**C** ☑ children should be reading more books.
**D** ☐ reading gossip magazines helps prepare children for today's world.

21. Some people argue that …

**A** ☑ it doesn't matter what children read, as long as they're reading.
**B** ☐ teenagers should only read online to help prepare them for the modern world.
**C** ☐ parents should make sure their children do not only read online.
**D** ☐ reading is all about books.

22. The author's attitude to reading can be described thus:

**A** ☑ Reading books is a unique process and should be encouraged.
**B** ☐ Reading is a rather old-fashioned way to pass on information.
**C** ☐ Reading is important, but it's more important for teenagers to participate in online life.
**D** ☐ Reading is the best way for young people to get involved in adult life.

23. The general attitude among young people as discovered by the survey seems to be that …

**A** ☐ reading is boring and useless.
**B** ☑ homework and school texts like Shakespeare's plays are very unpopular.
**C** ☐ the only books children read are fantasy novels.
**D** ☐ adults always complain too much about what children and teenagers read.

24. Choose the summary below which best applies to the text.

| | | | |
|---|---|---|---|
| **A** ☐ | The text is about the kind of books children have to read and about how much they dislike having to read these particular books. | **B** ☑ | The author describes the findings of a recent survey about the reading habits of children and teenagers, and talks briefly about different attitudes to reading. |
| **C** ☐ | The author writes about the reading habits in schools and how parents try to support their children's reading. | **D** ☐ | The text is about the psychological processes involved in reading, and how these processes differ between children and adults. |

## Part 5

| | A | | B | | C | | D | |
|---|---|---|---|---|---|---|---|---|
| 25 | ☑ | been | ☐ | be | ☐ | were | ☐ | being |
| 26 | ☐ | witch | ☐ | what | ☑ | which | ☐ | whose |
| 27 | ☑ | attach | ☐ | attack | ☐ | build | ☐ | hyperlink |
| 28 | ☐ | view | ☐ | understand | ☑ | open | ☐ | copy |
| 29 | ☑ | fit | ☐ | is fitting | ☐ | fits | ☐ | had fit |
| 30 | ☐ | think | ☐ | thinking | ☐ | thoughts | ☑ | thought |
| 31 | ☑ | at | ☐ | on | ☐ | to | ☐ | for |
| 32 | ☐ | entering | ☐ | entered | ☑ | enter | ☐ | entrance |
| 33 | ☐ | probably | ☑ | maybe | ☐ | likely | ☐ | impossibly |

# Writing

## Part 1

1. There are **too many** people coming this weekend, we don't have space for all of them.
2. My room **is (much) smaller** than my sister's!
3. The dining room is **in front of** the kitchen.
4. There is **a pair** of armchairs and a sofa in the living room.
5. There are doors **on either side/on both sides** of the bookshelves in the living room.

## Part 2

6. (Hi Mum,) On the way to school this morning Brian had a bike accident and hurt his leg really badly. I went to hospital with him. I'll go to school as soon as I know he's OK!
*(37 words)*

## Part 3

7. The last film I saw in the cinema was called *Twilight*. It's an American film about teenagers in Washington state. It rains a lot there. The film showed lots of beautiful landscapes, big mountains and forests and lakes, even though it rains all the time. The story was a bit slow, but the actors were very good; the plot is basically a love story between a young girl who moves to the town from another state, and a boy at her school who's actually a hundred-year-old vampire. Right at the end of the film there's a bit of action, too. *(100 words)*

8. When I finish school I want to take a year off and travel. There are lots of places I'd like to see all over the world, but I will probably have to stay in Europe because travelling to the US or Africa would be too expensive. I want to get some work experience and a better idea of the world and different cultures before I go to university to study. I would most like to study journalism or politics at university, and when I finish, I want to work for a national newspaper. *(93 words)*

## Listening: Tapescript

Track 5

## Part 1

0. MAN: Good evening, how can I help you?
WOMAN: Hello, I wanted to ask if there were any tickets left for the ballet this evening?
MAN: I'll have a look, but I think we should have a few tickets left. Let me see … Yes, yes, there are six tickets left – but standing room only, I'm afraid. Is that alright?
WOMAN: Oh, that's fine. Wonderful. Two tickets then, please.

1. MAN: Good morning, I wonder if you could help me. I have to fly to California next week, and I'm trying to find a cheap flight from Heathrow, if that's possible.
WOMAN: Hmm, you've left it rather late. I don't know if we can find a cheap flight on such short notice. Let's have a look. When exactly do you want to leave?
MAN: I have to be there on Thursday afternoon at the latest. So any time up to Wednesday night, I guess.
WOMAN: I see. It looks like the cheapest flight would leave on Tuesday afternoon from Heathrow, with a 12-hour stopover in Amsterdam. You would arrive in San Francisco early on Wednesday morning, local time. Altogether that would come to £435 – you are flying alone, aren't you?

2. This is an announcement for all passengers on the 7:16 train to Edinburgh. A flock of sheep has wandered onto the lines just north of London, and we're afraid that the train will be delayed until they can be moved off the tracks. We estimate a delay of forty-five minutes, and would like to apologise for the inconvenience.

3. WOMAN: Hello, I wonder if you could help me. I just arrived from London, and I wanted to change some money.
   MAN: No problem. Into euros?
   WOMAN: Yes, 60 pounds sterling into euros.
   MAN: Lovely. The exchange rate at the moment is quite good, you'll get €68,46 – minus our fee of € 15, of course.
   WOMAN: Fifteen euros! That's daylight robbery!

4. MAN: Have you finished packing yet, dear? Our taxi will be here in fifteen minutes.
   WOMAN: Oh, stop fussing, I'll be ready. Now, what do you think the weather will be like? Will we need our warm jumpers and coats, do you think?
   MAN: We're flying to Albuquerque – I seriously doubt we'll be needing warm coats in New Mexico in June.
   WOMAN: You never know, dear, you never know. I'll put in one set of warm clothes for each of us. Now, how about sports clothes – what do you think, that lovely cricket jumper I gave you for Christmas?
   MAN: Sports clothes? We're going on holiday, and I haven't played cricket since I was 11. Just pack our swimming costumes.

5. WOMAN: Hello, City Wide Taxis, how can I help?
   MAN: Yes, hello. I'd like to order a taxi please.
   WOMAN: Certainly sir. To which address?
   MAN: 26 Withers Lane, at seven o'clock this evening, please.
   WOMAN: Do you need any special services, sir? Wheelchair access, minivan, executive chauffeur service, limousine …
   MAN: Err, no. Just a taxi. That'd be great.

6. WOMAN: Hello, could I see your passport, please.
   MAN: Here you go.
   WOMAN: Please place your luggage here. Are you taking any hand baggage on board with you, sir?
   MAN: Just my briefcase.
   WOMAN: Did you pack your luggage yourself?
   MAN: Yes.
   WOMAN: Are you carrying anything for someone else, and has anyone else at any time placed anything in your luggage?
   MAN: No, and no.

## Part 2

Track 6

WOMAN: Good morning, Lulworth Cove Youth Hostel, how can I help you?
MAN: Good morning. I'd like to book a couple of rooms, please.
WOMAN: OK, let's see then. When do you want to come?
MAN: From the 14th to the 21st of June.
WOMAN: I see. We have some free rooms left in June, but not many. What did you need?
MAN: If possible, two family rooms.
WOMAN: Hmm. We have one family room and I can offer you two singles – or there's still space in the group rooms.
MAN: Oh, no – no group rooms. The family room and two singles will be fine. What do the rooms cost?
WOMAN: Adults pay £14 per night and children under 18 pay £10.95. Will you be wanting breakfast as well?
MAN: Does that cost extra?
WOMAN: Yes, that is a further £3.95 per person per day.
MAN: Oh. That will be quite expensive. Do I have to book that now as well, or can we decide later?
WOMAN: No problem, you can book the rooms now and let us know nearer the time whether you'll be wanting breakfast too.
MAN: Good, thanks. In that case I'd like to book the rooms now, please.
WOMAN: Certainly, sir. Under what name?
MAN: Jakob Römer.
WOMAN: Could you spell that, please?
MAN: J-A-K-O-B is my first name, and R-O-E-M-E-R is my surname.
WOMAN. OK. And the address?
MAN: Wins Strasse 52 – that's W-I-N-S and S-T-R-A-S-S-E, 10405 Berlin, Germany.
WOMAN: Is 10405 the postal code?
MAN: Yes, it is.
WOMAN: Great. And could I have a telephone number and/or an e-mail address, please?
MAN: Certainly. That's 0049 for Germany, then 30 for Berlin, and my number is 445 2121. The e-mail address is Jacob.Roemer@web.de. How can I pay? With credit card or by transfer?
WOMAN: Credit card would be fine.
MAN: OK, we can do that now, then. My number is … *(fade out)*

## Part 3

Track 7

My home town is called Christchurch, and it's on the south coast of England. You probably haven't heard of it – it's not a big place, and we don't have any world-famous museums or sport arenas here. But it's a very pretty place, and there are a lot of interesting things to do around here. If you're interested in the theatre, musicals, or concerts, then the Christchurch Arts Centre in the High Street is a good destination – there are events and performances every night of the week, all year round.
Near the Arts Centre you'll find the Historical Museum, which covers Christchurch's history back to its earliest days, when it was founded by the Saxons, up to recent times.

The town's harbour is a very important nature reserve, and is home to a large number of birds and plants which have become increasingly rare in England. The countryside around Christchurch is also very beautiful all along the south coast, and if you travel inland, it's not far to the New Forest, one of the most beautiful areas in south England.
There are a lot of water sports and other activities you can do along the coast around Christchurch, including surfing, fishing and boating.
But one of the oddest things in Christchurch has to be the Bicycle Museum – one of very few such museums worldwide, this museum was founded by a local lawyer in the 1970s, and has accumulated a collection of over 350 different kinds of bicycles, from all ages, including the famous British "Penny Farthing" bicycle and a large collection of custom models.
Christchurch is also twinned with various towns around the world and pupils from the local schools often participate in exchange programmes, for example with the town of Aalen in Germany.

Track 8

## Part 4

Radio presenter: Our studio guest today is a student from Burton Comprehensive School, who is going to talk to us about methods for preparing for exams. Everyone is nervous about taking exams, and sometimes that nervousness can make it difficult to study and prepare effectively. How do you prepare for exams and the stress of revision?

Studio guest: There are a number of things I try to do. The most important I find is not to get in a panic – that doesn't help at all. You have to try and stay calm, because you can't learn anything if you're worrying about stuff all the time. It helps to make a chart or schedule of what you have to revise. Keep to the schedule and make sure that you check off a topic once you've completed it. It's a simple psychological trick, but when you see every day that another item has been checked off and dealt with, you'll have a little boost of optimism about the whole business of revising.

Radio Presenter: How should this schedule be organised?

Studio Guest: Well, one important thing is to make sure that you have variety. I mean by that that you should under no circumstances have one full day on which you only revise maths topics, for example; make sure that you have a block of maths followed by something completely different – say, geography. And make sure that your learning blocks aren't too long: you'll all know this from school already, but it can't hurt to repeat it; no one can study for three hours and actually keep everything in their head.

Radio Presenter: That all makes sense. Any other tips for students?

Studio Guest: When you're studying foreign languages, it's important to get used to the sound of the language, so try and listen to French radio stations or podcasts on the Internet – or French-language pop music, if you want. And generally as a piece of advice for exams; they may look like a race against time, when you know that you only have two hours to finish a paper, but that time is going to be more than enough if you work carefully, patiently, and most importantly in an *unhurried* manner. Pretty much the worst thing you can do in an exam – apart from cheating or not turning up, of course – is to rush things. Take your time reading the tasks and questions, take your time thinking about how to answer, and take your time writing the answers.

RADIO PRESENTER: Thank you and good luck to everyone who has to take an exam anytime soon.

## Listening: Solutions

### Part 1

1. The man is at the airport shortly before the departure. What could be his flight?

A ☑

B ☐

C ☐

2. Why is the train delayed?

A ☐

B ☐

C ☑

3. How much money will the woman get in euros once she's exchanged the pounds for euros?

A ☐

B ☐

C ☑

4. What does the man think the woman should pack?

A ☐

B ☑

C ☐

5. What kind of service does the taxi company offer?

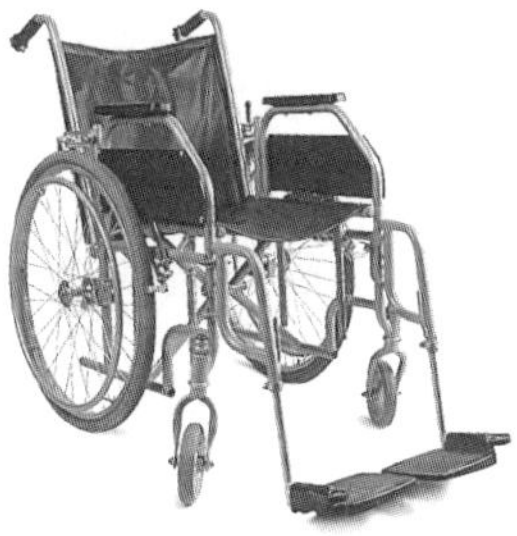

A ☑

B ☐

C ☐

6. What luggage is the passenger taking on board with him?

A ☐

B ☑

C ☐

## Part 2

7. The name of the youth hostel is Lulworth …
   - **A** ☑ Cove.
   - **B** ☐ Cave.
   - **C** ☐ Grove.

8. How long does the caller want to stay at the hostel?
   - **A** ☐ 21/06 to 04/07
   - **B** ☑ 14/06 to 21/06
   - **C** ☐ 04/06 to 21/06

9. How many rooms will the caller be booking?
   - **A** ☐ Two family rooms
   - **B** ☑ One family room and two singles
   - **C** ☐ Two single rooms

10. How much do children under 18 have to pay?
- **A** ☐ £14
- **B** ☐ £18.95
- **C** ☑ £10.95

11. Breakfast is …
- **A** ☐ not available.
- **B** ☑ available, but it costs extra.
- **C** ☐ included in the price of the rooms.

12. The caller gives his …
- **A** ☐ mobile phone number and e-mail address.
- **B** ☑ postal address and telephone number.
- **C** ☐ mobile phone number and office number.

## Part 3

**Christchurch**

Located: (13) *south* coast of England

Activities: (14) *Christchurch Arts Centre* in High Street: events (theatre, concerts) all year round

Sports: (15) *surfing*, (16) *fishing / boating* and other water sports.

Museums: (17) *Historical Museum* and (18) *Bicycle Museum*

## Part 4

| | A | B |
|---|---|---|
| 19. The studio guest has already finished school. | ☐ | ☑ |
| 20. It's important not to get in a panic about revising for exams. | ☑ | ☐ |
| 21. It helps to make a timetable of the subjects you have to study. | ☑ | ☐ |
| 22. Each study block should be at least two hours long to make sure you learn enough. | ☐ | ☑ |
| 23. If you study foreign languages, it is a good idea to listen to podcasts in this language. | ☑ | ☐ |
| 24. You won't have much time during the exams, so work as fast as possible. | ☐ | ☑ |

## Speaking

### Part 1

Possible conversation:

CANDIDATE A: What's your name?

CANDIDATE B: My name is …? What's your name?

CANDIDATE A: My name is …

CANDIDATE B: Oh, that's a difficult name. Can you spell that for me, please?

CANDIDATE A: Yes of course. It's spelled …

CANDIDATE B: Thank you. Where do you come from?

CANDIDATE A: I'm from … That's a small town near … Where are you from?

CANDIDATE B: I live in a big city, in … Do you like living in the country?

CANDIDATE A: Yes, I love it. We live in a big house where all my sisters and brothers have their own room. I couldn't imagine to share a room with one of them.

CANDIDATE B: How many sisters and brothers do you have?

CANDIDATE A: I've got two younger sisters and an older brother. What about you? Do you have any sisters or brothers?

CANDIDATE B: No, I don't, but I'd love to have an older brother. Sometimes it would be nice to have someone else to talk to at home, not only my parents. He could help me with my Maths homework, too …

CANDIDATE A: Well, I'm not sure you know what you're talking about. I'm always having arguments with my older brother. So I guess you don't like Maths?

CANDIDATE B: You're right, it's not my favourite subject. I prefer foreign languages, because I like travelling. Have you ever been abroad?

CANDIDATE A: Yes, I've been to Italy in the summer holidays. We went to Rome. It's a fascinating city, but after a few days I was fed up with sight-seeing.

…

### Part 2

CANDIDATE A: Now that we've looked at the four pictures, which one are you most interested in? Have you ever been to one of these countries before?

CANDIDATE B: Well, I think that's very hard to decide. I haven't been to any of these countries.

CANDIDATE A: If you don't know which country you would most like to visit, we can try and find out which country you don't want to go to. Do you like very hot weather?

CANDIDATE B: No, I can't stand too much heat. Then I can probably forget about Australia. And I don't like a lot of rain, so Scotland may be a bad choice for me, too.

CANDIDATE A: That leaves us with America and England. If you don't want to go too far away from where you live, then England would be better.

CANDIDATE B: Actually I would really like to go on a long-distance journey. That way I could see things we don't have in Europe

CANDIDATE A: Then of course you have to go to the USA.

## Part 3

CANDIDATE A: The picture I have is of a small, Asian-looking man with a big head, glasses, and dark hair. He is putting a piece of paper into a box – it looks like he is voting. The man is Kim Jong-Il, the leader of North Korea. Voting is usually typical of a democracy, but North Korea is not a democratic state. Kim Jong Il is a dictator and everybody has to obey him. In my opinion his appearance fits his role since he is wearing something like a uniform. His body language also suits a dictator: he looks very serious and does not look at the camera. I don't know much about North Korea – I don't think anybody does, do they? It's a very secretive country. North Korea is a Communist state, and it is very, very poor. They have arguments all the time with their neighbours, like Japan, and they are seen by the USA as being one of the most dangerous countries in the world. I don't really know much about Kim Jong-Il, but in my opinion he is hurting his own people by keeping them so poor and by always causing so much trouble with bigger, stronger countries that punish his country in response.

CANDIDATE B: The picture I was given is of Barack Obama, the President of the USA. I think you can see the Capitol in the background. Actually he is the first African American to become President of the United States. I guess you can say his biography is like the American Dream: you can make your dreams come true if you work hard. And the slogan he used during his election campaign is now known everywhere in the world: "Yes, we can." The picture also shows his character very well. He looks like a very friendly person but at the same time like someone who is sure of himself, someone who knows how to reach his goals. The fact that he smiles at the camera shows that he is interested in people. He uses the media to convince voters of his ideas and tries to win their sympathy. I think Barack Obama is a very popular leader, not only in the USA but also in Europe and many other countries. What is your opinion?

*(discussion between candidate A and B)*

## Part 4

CANDIDATE A: What about meeting next weekend and doing something together? I'd really love to see the new film with Brad Pitt. Why don't we meet Saturday afternoon at the cinema?

CANDIDATE B: I'm really sorry, but I can't. I'd like to see the film, too, but I've no more pocket money left this month. I've bought this new computer game and now I have to save money.

CANDIDATE A: A new computer game? Which one?

CANDIDATE B: It's called "The Olympic Games 2012". Maybe you like it, too. You could come to my house on Saturday afternoon and we could play together. We could also watch a DVD later on, a film with Brad Pitt if you like.

CANDIDATE A: That's a good idea! But I can't stay too long. I have to catch the bus at 8 p.m.

CANDIDATE B: My mum could drive you home. I'll ask her. When do you want to come? Maybe at 4 p.m.?

CANDIDATE A: That sounds good. There's a bus at a quarter to four. That should be no problem.

CANDIDATE B: Great, so see you on Saturday.

# Sprachenzertifikat Englisch B1
## *Mock Exam* 3

## Reading

### Part 1

*Read the texts and choose the correct explanation.*
*Tick (✓) the correct sentences and mark the letter (A–C) on your answer sheet.*
*There is an example at the beginning (0).*

0.

- ☑ **A** Only people who have given their details and received a password can use the e-mail on this website.
- ☐ **B** The website is open for use by anybody.
- ☐ **C** One password is shared by three people – they have to keep it secret!

1.

- ☐ **A** There are too many people here, you'll have to come back later.
- ☐ **B** When the number you have is shown on the display, it's your turn.
- ☐ **C** Wait your turn until you are given a number. Then take a seat.

2.

- ☐ **A** Get out of your car before it gets washed.
- ☐ **B** Don't leave your car once it's in the car wash.
- ☐ **C** Stay in your car until the wash begins.

3.

- ☐ **A** Because of the violence in this film children are not allowed to see it.
- ☐ **B** A 10-year-old is not allowed to see this film under any circumstances.
- ☐ **C** A 13-year-old can watch this film without his or her parents.

4. 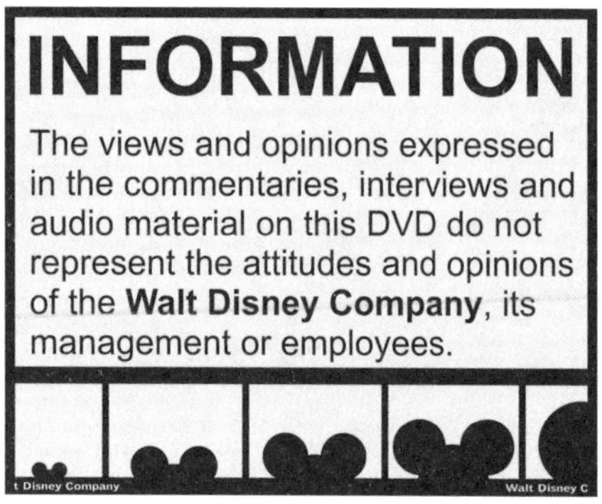


☐ **A** The Walt Disney Company is very angry about the opinions on this DVD.

☐ **B** This DVD was not made by the Walt Disney Company.

☐ **C** The Walt Disney Company does not want viewers to think that the ideas and opinions on the DVD reflect the Disney Company's own attitudes.

## Part 2

*People and jobs – Match these people (5–9) to the job ads (A–H) on the next pages.*

5. June wants to work with animals when she leaves school. She has always liked animals and although her father wants her to become a doctor, she would rather learn how to heal animals.

6. Jake likes things to be ordered, peaceful, and, above all – legal. He lives in a peaceful little town where there aren't many criminals, and he wants it to stay that way.

7. Mark has a good head for figures. He was always good at mathematics when he was at school, and he knows that if he can find a job involving maths, he'll do well – because most other people *don't* like maths, and aren't very good at it.

8. Anthony was taught to cook by his grandmother, but what he really wants is to be adored by millions of screaming teenagers … He was always the clown in his class, and he loves standing on stage and singing and dancing for other people.

9. Jeremy's father runs a restaurant in Yeovil, and he will work there when he's finished school. He loves to cook and he grew up in the kitchens of his father's restaurant. That's where he feels most at home. But his father wants him to get some experience working in other places, too.

A

**SUN LI**

Chinese Restaurant
in Church Street

寿司

We are looking for an apprentice to work in the kitchen. **No previous experience is necessary**, but we are looking for someone who is interested in cooking. You must be ready to work long hours in a **hot and very, very busy environment!**

Please send applications to
Mr Sun Li or

Help Wanted

call: 05698 2224

B

**Little Thrushwell Village Police**

**L. T. V. P.**

Little Thrushwell Village Police are looking for a trainee policeman or -woman. We offer a training environment for young people who are interested in joining the police force. Further information about specifications and requirements can be found on our website: **www.yorkshire_police.co.uk**

C

**Editor´s Assistant**

The magazine **Bournemouth Weekend** is looking for an assistant to the editor. We are looking for young people who have a talent for language and an orderly and methodical working approach. No previous experience in journalism is necessary, but we do need people who have a strong command of the English language and who are familiar with working with computers.

D

I am looking for a sharp-eyed young man or woman to work with me as an assistant. The work of a private detective requires sharp senses, concentration, discretion, and nerves of steel. If you have these qualities and are interested in working long hours, mostly at night, and aren't scared at the idea of getting into danger on a regular basis, then leave a piece of paper with your name and telephone number in the hole in the south wall of the old cemetery on Grosvenor Street.

Bart Barksley, Privat Detective

E

**Golden Evenings Retirement Home**

We are looking for a one-man or one-woman entertainment machine! If you love to have an audience and can sing, dance, play an instrument and keep people entertained for hours on end, then you should send us your application with complete references and copies of your qualifications. Write to: Mrs Edna Bright,
**34 Hillsborough Avenue, SP3 4DX, Salisbury**

Entertainment needed

F

Veterinary Clinic Looking for Clinic Assistant

We are looking for an assistant in the vet's clinic who can begin work immediately. Experience working with animals is essential, and we require any applicants who are younger than 18 to have the permission of their parents or guardians to assist in surgery on animals. Please remember that this work can sometimes involve very hard decisions! Please call Dr. Jim Bradley at 9898 556.

G

od Film Festival

**The Somerset Food Film Festival** is looking for a trainee for our press office. If you have a good telephone manner and are interested in film, working with the public, and food, then please apply!

Write to Emily Blunt at **e-blunt@somersetfff.co.uk** with your application and full CV.

Somerset Food Fil

H

# GOLDSACHS & GUPTA

The Financial Department of Goldsachs and Gupta Investment Bankers are looking for fresh new talent! We are a leading financial service provider, operating internationally from our offices in London. No previous experience in the finance sector is needed, but we do ask for applicants who have strong skills in mathematics and computing, and who are interested in the world of international finance. If you are interested, please send an application and CV to: **v.gupta@goldsachsgupta.co.uk**

| 5 | 6 | 7 | 8 | 9 |
|---|---|---|---|---|
| | | | | |

## Part 3

*After reading the flyer about working in Australia, decide if the statements are true or false. Tick (✓)* ***A*** *for* ***true*** *or* ***B*** *for* ***false****.*

| | A | B |
|---|---|---|
| 10. The agency offers work in Australia for up to three months. | ☐ | ☐ |
| 11. 'Tucker' and 'swag' mean accommodation and food. | ☐ | ☐ |
| 12. Lots of children in Australia can't get to schools, so they have to learn at home. | ☐ | ☐ |
| 13. You arrive in Australia at Melbourne International Airport. | ☐ | ☐ |
| 14. Shortly after you arrive, the first thing you do is spend three days relaxing on Rainbow Beach. | ☐ | ☐ |
| 15. The training courses are very full, so you'll be able to make lots and lots of new friends. | ☐ | ☐ |
| 16. The accommodation on the farm is usually in separate huts on the farm's property. | ☐ | ☐ |
| 17. The agency will provide help with the paperwork you need for your stay. | ☐ | ☐ |
| 18. You will need a passport which is valid for at least half a year. | ☐ | ☐ |
| 19. You won't need to take any money with you, because you'll be getting paid when you're there. | ☐ | ☐ |

# Have a working holiday in Australia!

Everybody loves Australia, with its huge landscapes, small population and amazing natural wonders. It's also a brilliant place to work and travel, and we offer guaranteed work there for up to a year. Time to prove we're not lazy Poms (what's a Pom? Well, they're the English)! Australians expect hard work and a positive attitude: in return you'll get a job for three to six months at the beginning, you'll be trained for the job, and you'll be paid around £ 180 per week, plus free tucker and a swag (OK, that means: a free place to sleep and free food).

**The work**
Generally, there are three main categories of work:
- Farming: hard physical work, looking after animals, repairing farm buildings, harvesting.
- Hospitality: in a hotel, restaurant, or pub (cooking, cleaning, waitressing)
- Teaching: if you like children, there are plenty of jobs for you – especially in the area of home schooling, which is still the only option for many kids in remote areas.

If you're a good rider, have worked on a farm, have ever done building work or worked as a secretary or cooked professionally, let us know – sometimes particular skills can help us find great job opportunities for you.

**How to get here**
When you arrive at Brisbane International Airport someone will come to meet you and will help you sort out your paperwork. And once that is dealt with, it's off to the beach for three days of relaxation! After that you will spend five days on a farm near Brisbane training for your work – this includes doing job interviews. You get to drive a tractor, ride a motorbike, work with cattle, repair cars, and work in the heat. Its hard work, but it's also a lot of fun, and you will make close friends: there will only be four of you on each training course.

**Accommodation**
You will stay on a farm, usually with the farmer's family. We ask you to be flexible: you might have to share a room. Accommodation and food are provided free of charge – and in return you are expected to be a friendly, helpful house guest.

**What is provided?**
- Interview and training, advice on how to do your paperwork in Australia
- Guaranteed paid work for the duration of your working visa
- 1 night accommodation in Brisbane, 3 nights accommodation at Rainbow Beach
- Food and accommodation at each stage
- Travel (by bus) to Rainbow Beach and to the training centre

**What do I need?**
- Passport valid for 6 months, Australian working holiday visa, insurance
- Cost of return flight to Brisbane (we can book for you), your travel costs to the airport, cost of travel from training farm to job, some money for the time when you are not working
- Appropriate clothing – **it's hot in Australia!**

## Part 4

*Here are some myths you've probably heard before, and maybe even believed – until now. After reading the text, answer the questions and mark the correct letter on your answer sheet.*

### Mythbusters

**MYTH: Marijuana is natural and therefore harmless.** But tobacco also grows naturally and has some very nasty effects. Tetrahydrocannabinol, or THC, is the chemical that causes some smokers to develop "tolerance" to its effects, and crave more of the drug, leading to addiction. Today's marijuana is on average twice as powerful as it was 20 years ago, and its effects and risks vary. Some is also laced with acid (LSD), PCP, or even includes chemicals like formaldehyde (yes, that's the stuff they put into dead bodies).

**MYTH: There are no long-term consequences if you smoke weed.** Smoking can lead to significant health, learning, and mental health problems, which can seriously ruin your future. It impairs judgment, which can lead to risky decisions when it comes to sex, driving, or doing things that would normally seem stupid to you, like illegal dares or practical jokes. It can dramatically affect your performance in school and in sports.

**MYTH: Magazine models are the ideal, and all women should look like them.** Did you know that the average American woman is actually 5 feet 4 inches tall (162 cm) and weighs 142 pounds (64 kg)? These days we are constantly being bombarded with images of the "perfect" man or woman. But take a look around – there are all sorts of successful, attractive, interesting people in the world, and they are all different sizes and shapes. Teenagers with low self-esteem are highly influenced by social pressure about body image, and may suffer from eating disorders that can have damaging effects on their bodies and their minds. And without treatment, up to 20 % of people with serious eating disorders die. With treatment, that number falls to 2–3 %. […]

**MYTH: Everyone in high school is having sex.** Actually, no – not everyone's "doing it", even if a lot of popular TV programmes make you think they are. Less than 50 % of US high school students report having ever had sex *(Centers for Disease Control DC)*. And the vast majority of teens (73 %) surveyed recently do not think it is embarrassing for teens to say they are virgins *(National Campaign to Prevent Teen Pregnancy)*. So whether you decide to wait because of the potential consequences, your beliefs, your parents' expectations, or just because you're not ready – you've made your decision, and your friends should respect that.

(adapted from: www.abovetheinfluence.com)

20. Marijuana can also …

**A** ☐ help overcome feelings of low self-esteem.

**B** ☐ help you study better.

**C** ☐ contain substances which are harmful to your health.

**D** ☐ help teenagers decide whether or not they want to have sex.

21. Smoking marijuana can have long-term consequences …

**A** ☐ because it's immediately addictive.

**B** ☐ because you can do silly things when under the influence which you may regret later.

**C** ☐ because you'll go to jail.

**D** ☐ because it makes you fat and unhealthy.

22. The average size of an American woman is …

**A** ☐ nearly 2 metres tall and less than 75 kg.

**B** ☐ very tall and quite thin.

**C** ☐ very short and very fat.

**D** ☐ just over 1½ metres, and less than 100 kg.

23. Pressures from society about the way bodies are perceived can …

**A** ☐ lead some teenagers to develop eating disorders.

**B** ☐ make everyone more aware of the importance of looking good and being fit.

**C** ☐ influence people to buy more fashion magazines.

**D** ☐ make teenagers turn to drugs and alcohol.

24. Choose the summary below which best applies to the text.

**A** ☐ The text is a collection of short pieces of information about the legal status of teenagers concerning certain issues, such as drugs and sexuality, and is written from an extremely conservative point of view.

**B** ☐ The text is a collection of brief pieces of advice for teenagers about how to deal with certain issues which affect adults, and helps them understand why grown-ups have trouble dealing with these issues.

**C** ☐ The text is a collection of very liberal opinions about teenagers and certain issues, such as drugs, sex and body image: the texts are anti-authoritarian, and would probably scare most teachers and parents with their pro-drug attitude.

**D** ☐ The text is a collection of brief responses to certain ideas about drugs and other issues which affect teenagers; the responses are trying to help readers understand how some widespread opinions about these issues are not true.

## Language Elements

*Read the text below; it is a letter of application.*
*To fill in the gaps decide which of the words (A–D) in the list below fits best.*
*There is an example at the beginning (0).*

(0) __________ Mr Bellamy,

After (1) _______ read the job vacancy announcement in last week's *Western Evening Chronicle*, I would like to apply for the job as assistant park supervisor for Bellamy Manor Park for the summer months of this year.

I have just completed my A-levels at Bellingham Comprehensive School and will be (2) _______ on to study Forestry Management at Manchester City University. I am (3) _______ with Bellamy Manor Park from many visits over the past few years, with my family and by myself. I have always been (4) _________ by the beauty of the park, as well as by the high level of maintenance and care that is obviously (5) __________ to keep the park in its current state. I have always been interested in the care of landscapes, gardens and the countryside, which is why I have chosen to (6) ___________ Forestry. For the past four years I have worked for (7) ___________ landscape gardening companies here in the area (8) ___________ the summer holidays, and also spent a month last year doing work experience with a forester in Scotland. The details of my relevant work experience can be found in the CV I have (9) ___________ with this letter.

The job interests me greatly, and I believe that I have the necessary qualifications and motivation to do well in it. Hopefully I will be considered for the post, and I would look forward to the chance of an interview for the position.

Yours (10) ___________,
Paul Lewis

| | | | | | | | | | | | | |
|---|---|---|---|---|---|---|---|---|---|---|---|---|
| 0 | **A** | ☐ | Yo! | **B** | ☐ | hey | **C** | ☑ | Dear | **D** | ☐ | Dearest |
| 1 | **A** | ☐ | being | **B** | ☐ | have | **C** | ☐ | has | **D** | ☐ | having |
| 2 | **A** | ☐ | going | **B** | ☐ | go | **C** | ☐ | gone | **D** | ☐ | goes |
| 3 | **A** | ☐ | family | **B** | ☐ | familiar | **C** | ☐ | popular | **D** | ☐ | familiarise |
| 4 | **A** | ☐ | influenced | **B** | ☐ | shocked | **C** | ☐ | impressed | **D** | ☐ | excited |
| 5 | **A** | ☐ | needed | **B** | ☐ | relevant | **C** | ☐ | require | **D** | ☐ | in need of |

| | | | | | | | | |
|---|---|---|---|---|---|---|---|---|
| 6 | **A** | ☐ do | **B** | ☐ teach | **C** | ☐ learn | **D** | ☐ study |
| 7 | **A** | ☐ various | **B** | ☐ varied | **C** | ☐ very | **D** | ☐ lot of |
| 8 | **A** | ☐ while | **B** | ☐ during | **C** | ☐ when | **D** | ☐ whilst |
| 9 | **A** | ☐ enclose | **B** | ☐ send | **C** | ☐ put in | **D** | ☐ included |
| 10 | **A** | ☐ sincerely | **B** | ☐ sincere | **C** | ☐ forever | **D** | ☐ truly |

## Writing

### Part 1

*Below are five sentences in which people are talking about things their friends have done. Complete the second sentence in each pair so that it means the same as the first sentence. You can use one to three words (and no more than three) to fill in the gaps. There is an example at the beginning (0).*

0. "Rob drove to Manchester with his parents last weekend."
Jeff ________________ Rob drove with his parents to Manchester last weekend.
*Answer sheet:* 0: said that

1. "Sheila wasn't too lucky at the concert last night, was she? She couldn't see a thing from where she stood!"
May says that Sheila ______________________ luck at the concert they went to last night, because she couldn't see anything.

2. "Jenny was absolutely furious about Dan. He totally ignored her all last night."
Nicky says that Jenny was very angry last night because Dan ______________________ to her the whole night.

3. "Naomi couldn't go to the cinema with us last night because she was really ill."
Richard said that Naomi ______________________ to go to the cinema because she had been feeling ill.

4. "Erik told me he spent all last night writing his blog and didn't get any of his homework done."
Ralph said that Erik told him he had ______________________ homework because he had been writing his blog all night.

5. "And then Terry was all like, 'Ow! I hurt myself!' and we were all looking at him lying on the floor, and it turned out he'd broken his arm."
Pete is telling someone that his friend Terry had ____________________ – he had broken his arm.

## Part 2

*Write a short e-mail (of 35–45 words) to a friend of yours who has missed school because they were ill.*

6. Ask your friend how he/she is feeling and explain what thc English homework is: to keep a diary in English for two weeks. Tell your friend that the teacher expects him/her to do the homework, too.

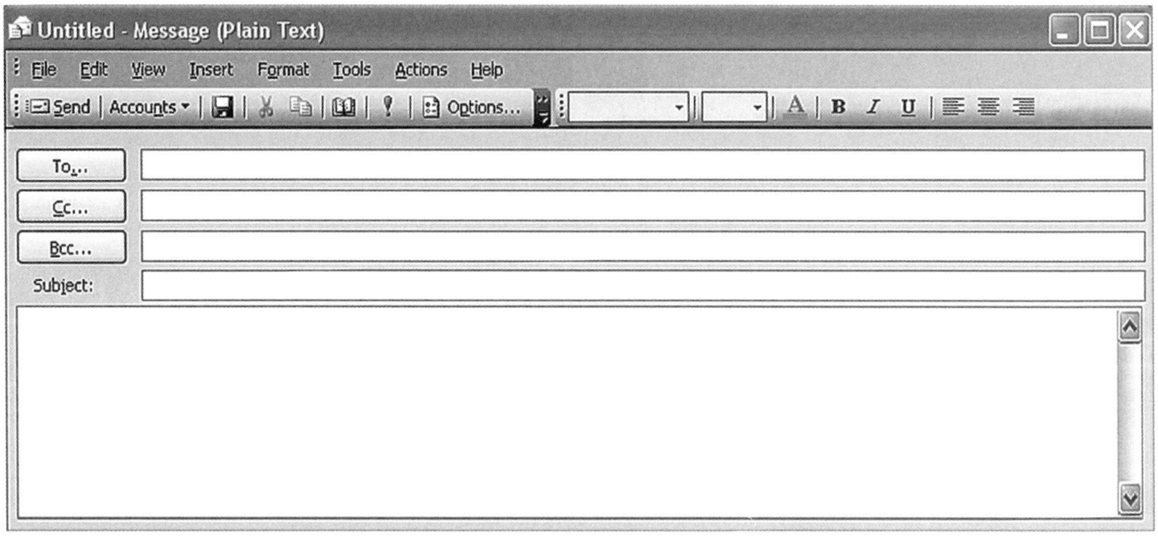


## Part 3

*Choose one of the two tasks 7 <u>or</u> 8 below and write a 100-word text.*
*Indicate which task you have chosen on your answer sheet.*

7. How do you keep yourself informed – newspapers, radio, TV, the Internet? Write a short text describing how you stay in touch with the world.

8. Write a short text about a historical figure who interests you.

## Listening

### Part 1

Track 9

*Listen to the short texts. Tick (✓) the correct picture and mark A, B or C on your answer sheet. There is an example at the beginning (0).*

0. Why don't they want to take the flat?

**A** ☐

**B** ☐

**C** ☑

1. What will the weather be like tomorrow?

**A** ☐

**B** ☐

**C** ☐

2. When might the meeting be over?

**A** ☐

**B** ☐

**C** ☐

3. How does the man know the news about Luigi's?

**A** ☐

**B** ☐

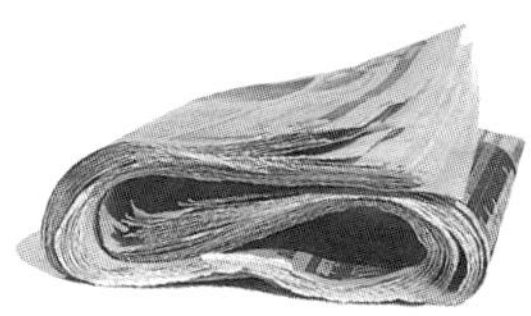
**C** ☐

4. What does the man think about the film?

**A** ☐

**B** ☐

**C** ☐

5. Where should the man NOT go on his way to the Town Hall?

**A** ☐

**B** ☐

**C** ☐

6. What does the woman order?

**A** ☐

**B** ☐

**C** ☐

Track 10

## Part 2

*You will hear a podcast about education issues in England.*
*Tick (✓) the correct box and mark A, B or C on your answer sheet.*

7. What did the survey study?
   - **A** ☐ Primary schools
   - **B** ☐ Comprehensive schools
   - **C** ☐ Schools in general

8. What example of alternative schooling is mentioned?
   - **A** ☐ Home schooling
   - **B** ☐ Boarding schools
   - **C** ☐ Military academies

9. At what age do English pupils usually start school?

**A** ☐ 4
**B** ☐ 5
**C** ☐ 6

10. Roughly how many pupils are now thought to be educated at home?

**A** ☐ 40,000
**B** ☐ 50,000
**C** ☐ 60,000

11. What is one reason mentioned in the article for the increased need for child care today?

**A** ☐ High unemployment
**B** ☐ Fears of children being forced to work
**C** ☐ More women are working the whole day

12. What do home-educated children do less of than school-educated pupils?

**A** ☐ Watching TV
**B** ☐ Doing sports
**C** ☐ Playing outdoors

## Part 3

Track 11

*Someone is talking about work experience.*
*Look for the missing information and fill in the gaps.*

**Work experience**

The man's opinion about the difference between …

… work: (13) ______________________________ *(one aspect)*

… and work experience: (14) ______________________________ *(one aspect)*

How to get work experience: ask family members, go to your (15) ______________________

at school, write a (16) __________ and a letter of application.

What to do before an interview: (17) ______________________________ *(one aspect)*

Golden Rule during your work experience: (18) ______________________________

## Part 4

Track 12

*Read the statements below, then listen to two people who are working in a book shop. Decide if the statements are true or false. Tick (✓) A for* ***true*** *and* ***B*** *for* ***false****.*
*Mark the correct letter on your answer sheet.*

| | A | B |
|---|---|---|
| 19. The Crime section is going to be left where it is. | ☐ | ☐ |
| 20. One of the most popular sections in the bookshop is the Crime section. | ☐ | ☐ |
| 21. Cookery and Gardening are going to be moved together. | ☐ | ☐ |
| 22. The Children's book section is not going to be moved, just changed around. | ☐ | ☐ |
| 23. There are five people doing work experience at the bookshop. | ☐ | ☐ |
| 24. All the changes are going to be made tomorrow. | ☐ | ☐ |

# Speaking

## Part 1

*In the oral exam there are usually two candidates, an interlocutor and an examiner who observes the conversations. In the first part of the exam the interlocutor asks each candidate about personal details, everyday life, hobbies etc. Or else you are asked to talk to each other. Have a look at mock exams 1 and 2 for possible questions.*

## Part 2

*We are going to describe a situation to you both. You'll then talk to each other to discuss the topic. There are some pictures to give you ideas.*
*The topic for this section is: Feelings.*
*Look at the pictures of the people, and think about what feelings they represent. Talk to each other and exchange ideas about what you see in the pictures.*

## Part 3

*Each of you is now going to be given a photograph. Both photographs are of people dancing. I want you both to take a minute to look at the photograph, because you are going to be asked to describe your photographs to each other.*
*Candidate A will start – Candidate B, just listen and then it's your turn.*
*When you are looking at your photographs, think about the kind of language you will need to describe what you see. Think about things like:*

- *Which country or culture do these dances come from?*
- *What kind of situation did this dance take place in?*
- *Are you familiar with either kind of dancing? What do you know about these dance styles?*

Photograph Candidate A:

Photograph Candidate B:

## Part 4

*Your pictures both showed different kinds of dancing. Each of you will now use both photographs to talk briefly about what you know and think about the dance styles – when they were popular, who dances like this, and in what circumstances, whether the dances are difficult or easy, whether you need to be trained to do them, whether they are dances that are available to all kinds of people, or just to certain sections of the population. Now discuss.*

# Lösungsvorschläge

## Reading

### Part 1

1. **A** ☐ There are too many people here, you'll have to come back later.
   **B** ☑ When the number you have is shown on the display, it's your turn.
   **C** ☐ Wait your turn until you are given a number. Then take a seat.

2. **A** ☑ Get out of your car before it gets washed.
   **B** ☐ Don't leave your car once it's in the car wash.
   **C** ☐ Stay in your car until the wash begins.

3. **A** ☐ Because of the violence in this film children are not allowed to see it.
   **B** ☐ A 10-year-old is not allowed to see this film under any circumstances.
   **C** ☑ A 13-year-old can watch this film without his or her parents.

4. **A** ☐ The Walt Disney Company is very angry about the opinions on this DVD.
   **B** ☐ This DVD was not made by the Walt Disney Company.
   **C** ☑ The Walt Disney Company does not want viewers to think that the ideas and opinions on the DVD reflect the Disney Company's own attitudes.

### Part 2

| 5 | 6 | 7 | 8 | 9 |
|---|---|---|---|---|
| F | B | H | E | A |

### Part 3

| | A | B |
|---|---|---|
| 10. The agency offers work in Australia for up to three months. | ☐ | ☑ |
| 11. 'Tucker' and 'swag' mean accommodation and food. | ☑ | ☐ |
| 12. Lots of children in Australia can't get to schools, so they have to learn at home. | ☑ | ☐ |
| 13. You arrive in Australia at Melbourne International Airport. | ☐ | ☑ |
| 14. Shortly after you arrive, the first thing you do is spend three days relaxing on Rainbow Beach. | ☑ | ☐ |
| 15. The training courses are very full, so you'll be able to make lots and lots of new friends. | ☐ | ☑ |

| | | |
|---|---|---|
| 16. The accommodation on the farm is usually in separate huts on the farm's property. | ☐ | ☑ |
| 17. The agency will provide help with the paperwork you need for your stay. | ☑ | ☐ |
| 18. You will need a passport which is valid for at least half a year. | ☑ | ☐ |
| 19. You won't need to take any money with you, because you'll be getting paid when you're there. | ☐ | ☑ |

**Part 4**

20. Marijuana can also …

**A** ☐ help overcome feelings of low self-esteem.
**B** ☐ help you study better.
**C** ☑ contain substances which are harmful to your health.
**D** ☐ help teenagers decide whether or not they want to have sex.

21. Smoking marijuana can have long-term consequences …

**A** ☐ because it's immediately addictive.
**B** ☑ because you can do silly things when under the influence which you may regret later.
**C** ☐ because you'll go to jail.
**D** ☐ because it makes you fat and unhealthy.

22. The average size of an American woman is …

**A** ☐ nearly 2 metres tall and less than 75 kg.
**B** ☐ very tall and quite thin.
**C** ☐ very short and very fat.
**D** ☑ just over 1½ metres, and less than 100 kg.

23. Pressures from society about the way bodies are perceived can …

**A** ☑ lead some teenagers to develop eating disorders.
**B** ☐ make everyone more aware of the importance of looking good and being fit.
**C** ☐ influence people to buy more fashion magazines.
**D** ☐ make teenagers turn to drugs and alcohol.

24. Choose the summary below which best applies to the text.

| | | | |
|---|---|---|---|
| A ☐ | The text is a collection of short pieces of information about the legal status of teenagers concerning certain issues, such as drugs and sexuality, and is written from an extremely conservative point of view. | B ☐ | The text is a collection of brief pieces of advice for teenagers about how to deal with certain issues which affect adults, and helps them understand why grown-ups have trouble dealing with these issues. |
| C ☐ | The text is a collection of very liberal opinions about teenagers and certain issues, such as drugs, sex and body image: the texts are anti-authoritarian, and would probably scare most teachers and parents with their pro-drug attitude. | D ☑ | The text is a collection of brief responses to certain ideas about drugs and other issues which affect teenagers; the responses are trying to help readers understand how some widespread opinions about these issues are not true. |

## Language Elements

| | | | | |
|---|---|---|---|---|
| 1 | A ☐ being | B ☐ have | C ☐ has | D ☑ having |
| 2 | A ☑ going | B ☐ go | C ☐ gone | D ☐ goes |
| 3 | A ☐ family | B ☑ familiar | C ☐ popular | D ☐ familiarise |
| 4 | A ☐ influenced | B ☐ shocked | C ☑ impressed | D ☐ excited |
| 5 | A ☑ needed | B ☐ relevant | C ☐ require | D ☐ in need of |
| 6 | A ☐ do | B ☐ teach | C ☐ learn | D ☑ study |
| 7 | A ☑ various | B ☐ varied | C ☐ very | D ☐ lot of |
| 8 | A ☐ while | B ☑ during | C ☐ when | D ☐ whilst |
| 9 | A ☐ enclose | B ☐ send | C ☐ put in | D ☑ included |
| 10 | A ☑ sincerely | B ☐ sincere | C ☐ forever | D ☐ truly |

## Writing

### Part 1

1. May says that Sheila **had no/bad** luck at the concert they went to last night, because she couldn't see anything.

2. Nicky says that Jenny was very angry last night because Dan **did not talk/speak** to her the whole night.

3. Richard said that Naomi **wasn't able** to go to the cinema because she had been feeling ill.

4. Ralph said that Erik told him he had **not done his/any** homework because he had been writing his blog all night.

5. Pete is telling someone that his friend Terry had **hurt himself** – he had broken his arm.

## Part 2

6.

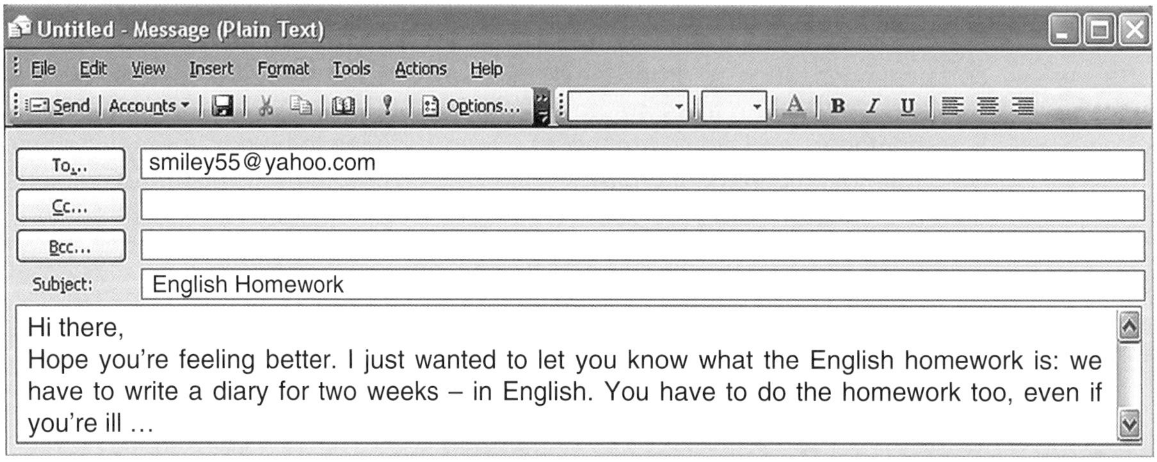


*(40 words)*

## Part 3

7. At home in our family we have the radio on every morning, so I always hear some of the news that way. My dad always reads a newspaper, but I usually only look at the pages about what's on TV or reviews of films and concerts. When I want to find out about what's going on in the world I usually look at the websites of international media companies like the BBC or CNN. And then in the evening we sometimes watch the news at 8 o'clock, but not every day. The Internet is much more up to date. *(99 words)*

8. One of the historical figures I find most interesting is King Henry VIII of England. He was a very lively character who encouraged the growth of culture in England and who also had very strong opinions about how to run the country. These opinions were not always popular in the rest of Europe, and he had arguments with the Pope about the Catholic religion. He wasn't allowed to marry the woman he wanted to, so he created his own church – the Church of England. Then he could finally get a divorce. He was married a total of six times.

*(99 words)*

## Listening: Tapescript

Track 9

### Part 1

0. MAN: So, what do you think of the flat?
   WOMAN: It's very nice. It really is. The rooms are big, the ceilings are high, it gets a lot of light …
   MAN: But?
   WOMAN: It's just that it's on the fourth floor. And there's no lift.
   MAN: Yes, that might get tiring after a while.
   WOMAN: And also – I mean, it's Sunday today, so everything is very quiet, but look out of the back window – there's a factory over there behind the garden. If we were to come back tomorrow, I'm sure things would be a *lot* louder here.

1. Here's the weather report for west Dorset for tonight and tomorrow. We're looking at some heavy rainfall expected for tonight, with strong winds from the north east and storm warnings for coastal areas. The winds will let up by morning, but expect heavy rainfall moving across the region from east to west right through tomorrow. The bad weather will let up by the afternoon, with the chance of seeing the sun by early evening.

2. MAN: B & B Real Estate, this is Stephen speaking, how may I help you?
   WOMAN: Hello Stephen, this is Mrs Wright. Is my husband in?
   MAN: Hello Mrs Wright, I'm afraid he's in a meeting at the moment. Should I ask him to call you back?
   WOMAN: When do you think he'll be finished?
   MAN: It's quite an important meeting with some business partners from Japan. I imagine he'll be in there until six at the earliest.
   WOMAN: Oh, I see. In that case don't worry, it's not that urgent. I'll see him later anyway.

3. MAN: I really don't want to cook tonight, shall we go out for dinner?
   WOMAN: That sounds good. Where do you want to go?
   MAN: I thought of trying out that new Sri Lankan place on the high street. Or maybe Luigi's.
   WOMAN: Ugh – not Luigi's. That meal I had last time we were there was *awful*.
   MAN: But I read in the local section of the paper that he'd got a whole new kitchen staff – I'm sure that was just a one-off stroke of bad luck. Come on, let's try his restaurant again.

4. WOMAN: That was a wonderful film. Don't you think?
   MAN: Bits of it. I liked the bit right at the beginning, just before it started, and I also really liked the bit right at the end when the lights came back on and we could go. The long bit in the middle when I was asleep was also OK.
   WOMAN: That's the very last time I go to the cinema with you.

5. Man: Hello, excuse me, could you help me? I'm trying to get to the Town Hall.
   Woman: Let me see. Follow this street down to the crossing and take a left into Church Street, and carry on until you get to the river. Turn right before the bridge and head up Nelson Street until you get to the roundabout. You need to take the third exit into Gibson Street. Then it's just a short way along until you get to the park. The Town Hall is to the left of the park.
   Man: I see. Thank you very much.

6. Man: Pizza Kings, good evening, how can I help you?
   Woman: Good evening, I'd like to place an order please.
   Man: OK, what'll it be?
   Woman: I'd like one Hawaii pizza, family size, with extra pineapple; one large salami and pepperoni pizza with extra pepperoni; and four cans of Coke. Oh, and one mixed salad please.
   Man: Sorry, we don't have any salad left.
   Woman: OK, then without the salad.
   Man: That'll be £21.75 and it'll take about forty minutes. What name shall I put on the order?

## Part 2

Track 10

Welcome to the latest Radio Somerset education podcast. As part of our current series on education issues here on Radio Somerset, we're going to present the results of a study conducted by academics as part of a Cambridge University study of primary schools in England. The report, which was published earlier this month, claims that parents are increasingly turning to alternative forms of education, such as home schooling, in order to save their children from the strict regime of frequent testing and targets in state schools. English pupils are among the youngest in the world when it comes to starting learning at school – usually around the age of four. During their time in the education system, they're also tested more often than pupils of almost any other country. The pressure placed on children due to this punishing system is apparently alarming parents, the report suggests. Many parents are now considering alternative forms of education. The most common reaction is to start teaching at home. Another course taken is to send their children to alternative schools, in which learning is loosened by play and creative work, lessening the pressures on pupils. It's thought that around 50,000 children are now being educated at home, a massive increase over the past few years.

The school starting age in England is legally five – but most children now start at age four. According to the study, one of the major factors is the rising need for child care as more women are now working full-time. The school starting age of five was introduced in 1870 to stop children being used as cheap labour, and it hasn't changed since then.

The area that concerns parents most, however, is the testing. No other country seems to be so concerned with national standards – but parents who have gone through this experience are now supported by the new study, that home-taught children do better in exams. And – much to everyone's surprise – home-educated pupils are less likely to spend hours watching TV or playing on computers.

Thank you for downloading Radio Somerset education podcast. We hope you'll join us again for the next edition later this week.

## Part 3

Track 11

Is there a difference between work and work experience? Yes, of course there is – work means moaning about your boss, taking a lot of coffee breaks, and stealing things from the supply cupboard. And you get paid for all of that. Work experience on the other hand means being enthusiastic, hard-working, and full of ideas, while not earning a penny and never complaining. The point of work experience is that it leads to work, and all its benefits. The best way to get work experience is through nepotism – that is, a relative or a friend of your family will promise to get you a good position in the place where they work. They'll forget about this promise and be totally surprised when you turn up for your first day – and they'll quickly get someone else to look after you. And that "good position"? That will probably turn out to be either filing – spending hours in a small room with no windows putting mountains of paper into the correct drawers – or you'll be told to wait in a corner. And wait. And wait … Another way to get work experience is to ask the careers officer in your school, who will help you write a CV and a covering letter to help you get an interview. But whichever path you choose, it would be best if you knew beforehand what you want from your work experience – what kind of work do you want to learn more about? What do you think you'll be doing in the future? What kind of company do you want to work for? It's also a good idea to get to know more about the place you're going to be working once you know where it is: look at the company's website, check out the competition, and then you'll be able to show off in your interview. It's a good idea to apply to places which have a recognized work experience programme – English companies normally have an award from the National Council for Work Experience. These companies will know how to deal with you – and they'll also be interested in treating you properly and helping you learn, and not wasting your time (or their own). Other companies may be more interested in getting some free labour than in helping you develop yourself. During your work experience, there's one Golden Rule – never be afraid to ask questions! You're there to learn, and it's no good to you if you don't understand how or why everything around you is being done. Take notes if you want, and learn from your mistakes. And at the end, make sure you ask for feedback.

## Part 4

Track 12

**Changing shelves in the bookshop**

Man: So, today I decided we're going to move some things around in here. I'd like to put the Crime section over on the back wall on the right, next to Science Fiction, and put the New Titles here on the left where the customers come in.

Woman: Why are we putting Crime at the back of the shop? It's one of the best-selling sections we have.

Man: Exactly, there's no need to put it up front, the customers will always find it. It doesn't need to be pushed at all. Now this section – Cookery and Travel – this needs some pushing. We'll put this whole section to the right of the counter, there's enough space.

Woman: It has a lot of space, that's true. We can display the big cook books better there.

MAN: Indeed. And the narrow shelf there to the left would be good for the maps; we just need to write some labels to organise them alphabetically by country.

WOMAN: How about the Children's Book section?

MAN: I don't want to move that to another spot in the shop, it's fine where it is – but we have to change it a bit. Customers are always excited by changes in shops they know.

WOMAN: The easiest thing to do would be to just swap everything around: put the Young Adult fiction and the Children's Non-Fiction on the left, and put the Toddler and Baby Books on the right.

MAN: Good idea. That won't take long. OK – as soon as the work experience kids get in, get two of them to start moving the children's section around, and I'll take the other two to begin work on moving Crime and New Titles. We have a busy day ahead of us!

## Listening: Solutions

### Part 1

1. What will the weather be like tomorrow?

A ☑

B ☐

C ☐

2. When might the meeting be over?

A ☐

B ☐

C ☑

3. How does the man know the news about Luigi's?

A ☐

B ☐

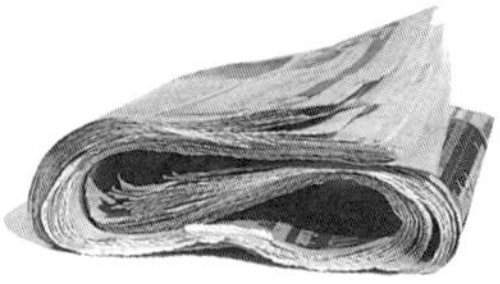
C ☑

4. What does the man think about the film?

**A** ☑

**B** ☐

**C** ☐

5. Where should the man NOT go on his way to the Town Hall?

**A** ☐

**B** ☑

**C** ☐

6. What does the woman order?

**A** ☐

**B** ☑

**C** ☐

## Part 2

7. What did the survey study?
   - **A** ☑ Primary schools
   - **B** ☐ Comprehensive schools
   - **C** ☐ Schools in general

8. What example of alternative schooling is mentioned?
   - **A** ☑ Home schooling
   - **B** ☐ Boarding schools
   - **C** ☐ Military academies

9. At what age do English pupils usually start school?

**A** ☑ 4
**B** ☐ 5
**C** ☐ 6

10. Roughly how many pupils are now thought to be educated at home?

**A** ☐ 40,000
**B** ☑ 50,000
**C** ☐ 60,000

11. What is one reason mentioned in the article for the increased need for child care today?

**A** ☐ High unemployment
**B** ☐ Fears of children being forced to work
**C** ☑ More women are working the whole day

12. What do home-educated children do less of than school-educated pupils?

**A** ☑ Watching TV
**B** ☐ Doing sports
**C** ☐ Playing outdoors

## Part 3

**Work experience**

The man's opinion about the difference between …

… work: (13) *taking coffee breaks / moaning about the boss*
*stealing office supplies* *(one aspect)*

… and work experience: (14) *being enthusiastic / full of ideas* *(one aspect)*

How to get work experience: ask family members, go to your (15) *careers officer*
at school, write a (16) *CV* and a letter of application.

What to do before an interview: (17) *look at the company's website / check out the competition*
*(one aspect)*

Golden Rule during your work experience: (18) *never be afraid to ask questions*

## Part 4

| | A | B |
|---|---|---|
| 19. The Crime section is going to be left where it is. | ☐ | ☑ |
| 20. One of the most popular sections in the bookshop is the Crime section. | ☑ | ☐ |
| 21. Cookery and Gardening are going to be moved together. | ☐ | ☑ |
| 22. The Children's book section is not going to be moved, just changed around. | ☑ | ☐ |
| 23. There are five people doing work experience at the bookshop. | ☐ | ☑ |
| 24. All the changes are going to be made tomorrow. | ☐ | ☑ |

# Speaking

## Part 1

Mögliche Antworten zu diesem Teil findest du in den Lösungen zu *Mock Exams* 1 und 2.

## Part 2

CANDIDATE A: There are six photographs of people which show different feelings. One picture shows a boy sitting with his head in his hands and adults shouting at each other in the background. They are obviously angry, and he looks very upset.

CANDIDATE B: It looks like this is a family argument and that the child is suffering because his parents fight all the time. Another picture illustrates frustration and anger: a man is shouting at his laptop.

CANDIDATE A: Perhaps his laptop is not working correctly and he is under pressure to finish an important piece of work. The picture of the boy at the bottom of the page clearly shows feelings of triumph and happiness – someone has won something.

CANDIDATE B: Or his favourite football team has just won an important match. Above there is a picture of young people dancing in what seems to be a club or a disco. The emotions shown in this picture are happiness and excitement: the people we can see are smiling and laughing and dancing.

CANDIDATE A: And there's another picture which shows positive emotions. The girl on the left wears the typical dress of graduation day. She seems to be very proud of her diploma. The last picture shows a more unhappy subject.

CANDIDATE B: Yes, it shows a woman sitting by herself and looking at nothing. She seems to be unhappy, and the fact that she is alone might mean that she is lonely, that she misses someone, or that she is unhappy because someone is not with her.

CANDIDATE A: In the background you can see graves. Maybe she has just lost a beloved person and now she is visiting his or her grave.

## Part 3

CANDIDATE A: My picture shows a traditional style of dancing. A couple is dancing together. The woman's dress and the way they are holding each other makes me think of dances like flamenco or tango. But the picture could also represent ballroom dancing in general. Ballroom dancing is very formal and the dancers have to dress and move in very specific ways. It is something you have to practise and work at, and you can't do it by yourself – it has to be done with a partner or in a group. There are ballroom dancing competitions, and I guess that the people who do it take it very seriously. The couple in the picture also look as if they were professionals or at least people who are very enthusiastic about their hobby. I have been to a beginners' class of ballroom dancing and I must say that it is much harder than it looks. I gave up after the first class, however, because I didn't like the music. I prefer dancing on my own at a club to dancing in couples.

CANDIDATE B: As you said, the first picture shows a traditional style of dance and my picture is a contrast to this. It shows someone break dancing. This is also a kind of dancing which requires a lot of work: it's very athletic and needs a lot of practice. Break dancing is part of the hip-hop culture. I think it was developed in the USA. The clothes are also important in break dancing, but there is more freedom in how you dress than there is in ballroom dancing. Break dancing is less formal than ballroom dancing – you don't need to reserve a large room, or have an audience, or do it in groups. All you need is music, space on the floor and room to move around. I am not personally familiar with either kind of dance – I've never done ballroom dancing, and I can't break dance.

## Part 4

I don't know much about this formal style of dancing, and I'm not very interested in it. I've only seen it in films or on TV, and I really don't like the kind of music they dance to. I don't understand why they all have to do the same thing all the time – there is no freedom in how they can dance or dress. It also seems to me that there is far too much discipline in it. Shouldn't dancing be about being free and expressing yourself?

Break dancing also needs a lot of discipline, but it is all about self-expression. You have to try and do better moves than the other break dancers. In break dancing it's important to invent new moves to impress other dancers – so you have to be really creative, which is very different from the ballroom dancing in the other picture. Because ballroom dancing is so complicated, it's definitely not something you can do when you feel like it: it needs a lot of preparation, and is probably actually very expensive, because you need to be trained, you need those strange clothes, and you need to hire or rent rooms to practise in or you have to join a club. It's a kind of dancing which I think is only liked or done by rich or privileged people. Break dancing is a much more "democratic" kind of dancing – it's from the street, and it is meant to be something that can be done by anybody who wants to do it and is prepared to work at it. You don't need money to do it, and the whole idea of break dancing is more about being an individual and expressing yourself than just obeying a strict tradition, like with ballroom dancing.

## Sprachenzertifikat Englisch B1
## *Mock Exam* 4

## Reading

### Part 1

*Read the texts and choose the correct explanation.*
*Tick (✓) the correct sentences and mark the letter (A–C) on your answer sheet.*
*There is an example at the beginning (0).*

0.

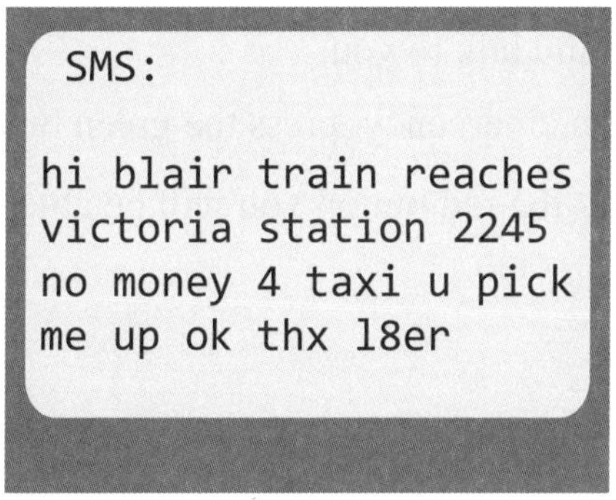


- ☑ **A** Hello Blair, my train reaches Victoria Station at a quarter to eleven at night. I have no money for a taxi, could you please pick me up? Thanks – see you later
- ☐ **B** The train from Blair reaches Victoria Station at ten forty-five p.m., send a taxi to pick me up if you're going to be late
- ☐ **C** If you don't have any money to send a taxi when my train reaches Victoria Station, please come and pick me up. See you later

1.

- ☐ **A** People find it offensive to drink alcohol here.
- ☐ **B** It is illegal to drink alcohol in public here.
- ☐ **C** Alcohol is free in this area.

2.

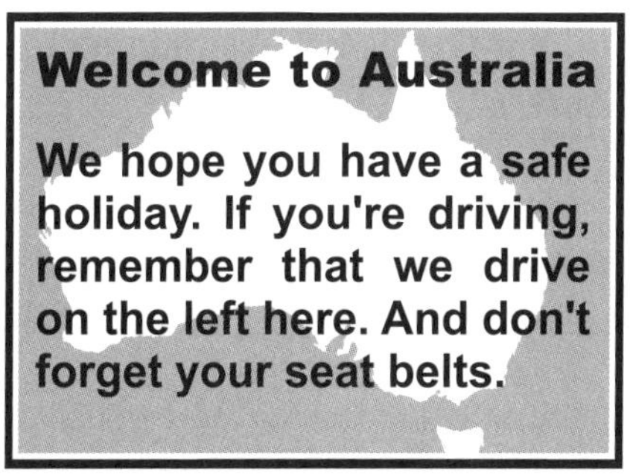


- ☐ **A** Australians don't drive on the right-hand side of the road.
- ☐ **B** You have to bring your own seat belts with you when you go to Australia.
- ☐ **C** You shouldn't drive when you're on holiday in Australia.

3.

☐ **A** You are not allowed to take luggage which is heavier than 20 kg.

☐ **B** You can charge extra if your baggage is heavier than 20 kg.

☐ **C** You will have to pay extra if you are bringing luggage which is heavier than 20 kg.

4.
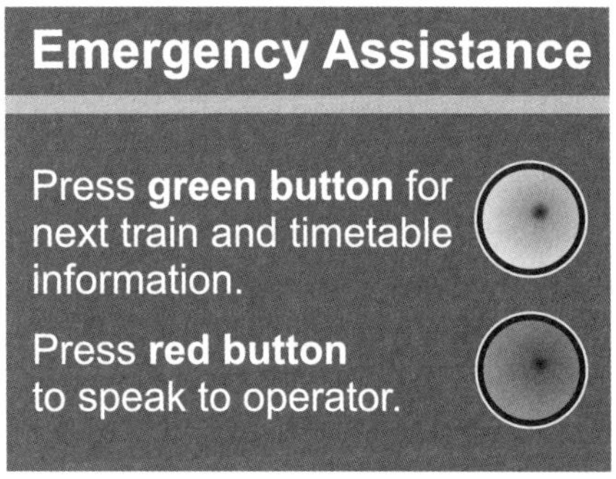


☐ **A** If you press the green button, the next train will come; if you press the red button, the operator will come and talk to you.

☐ **B** If there's an emergency, press the green button.

☐ **C** If you press the red button you will be able to talk to the operator.

## Part 2

*These people are looking for different things when they go on holiday.*
*Match the people (5–9) to the ads (A–H) below. There are more ads than you need.*

5. When Uncle Tim goes on holiday to Scotland, he likes to go to military history museums. When he was in the army he knew a few soldiers from the Highland Regiments, and he was very impressed by their courage and discipline.

6. My older brother really loves ruins and old castles. Whenever we go on holiday, he always reads up beforehand about the history of the place we're going to – especially about the Middle Ages.

7. My dad may be old, but he still loves active holidays – water sports, running, cycling tours. It's quite exhausting. I prefer to lie on the beach and read, but Dad is always running up and down the beach looking for a place where he can rent a surfboard …

8. My sister looks for culture when she's on holiday. She loves going to the theatre, to operas, to museums, art galleries – that kind of thing. She wants to work in museums when she's older, and she's already started studying Art History at university.

9. My mother says that the reason she likes to travel is to see spectacular natural phenomena. She doesn't care for museums or galleries and she hates sports, and she gets bored very quickly if we spend time on the beach, so she will normally go on her own and take a bus to find the kind of landscapes we don't have at home.

A

NIAGARA FALLS

**The most spectacular – The loudest – The wettest – The most thrilling**
One of the most famous natural wonders in the world! Come to Niagara Falls on the Canadian-US border! Plenty of opportunities for sightseeing, eating, staying the night, and travelling in the area!

B

Canadian Adventure
HOLIDAYS FOR CHILDREN

Contact
Brian Greggs
b_greggs@caahc.ca

We offer thrilling opportunities for children under 18 to experience the wilderness of Canada – camping out in the forests, mountain-climbing for beginners, even bear-watching in the National Parks. Take a canoe trip, climb down into dark tunnels under the mountains, see magnificent scenery and experience the majesty of the Canadian wilds!

C

**Edinburgh Military Museum**

Enjoy the finest collections of our national military history. With uniforms from throughout the ages, many informative guides to Scottish history, and thousands of portraits and photographs in our gallery.
*Open Monday to Saturday from 10 to 4. Guided tours available.*
*Group discounts available on request.*

D

**JET SKI HIRE**

In the summer months every day from 7 a.m. until 8 in the evening – experienced trainers can help beginners. Speed boat pilots are ready to take you out onto the waves. Enjoy the speed and excitement of being dragged through the water at 300 miles per hour!

**Ask at Jet Ski Hire on South Beach.**

E

DECK CHAIR WARRIORS

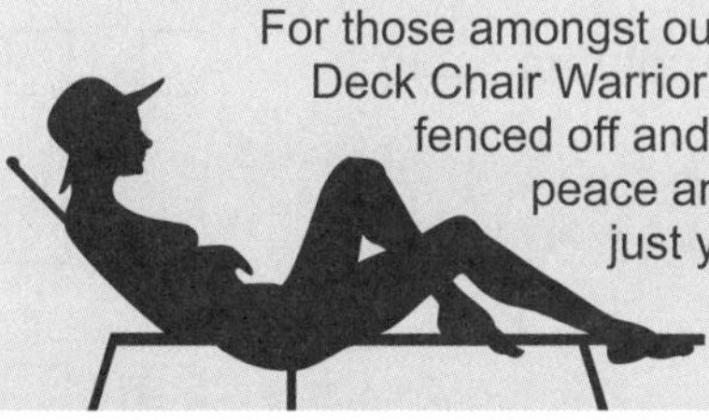

For those amongst our guests who like it slow and relaxed on holiday, we provide a special Deck Chair Warrior service – an exclusive, separate area of the South Beach has been fenced off and is dedicated to the slow style of holidaying. Deck chairs, sun screens, peace and quiet – no screaming children, no loud youths, no irritated parents – just you, the sun, the sand, and a book or sleep. Paradise has never been so close! **Please ask at the DCW cabin, at the entrance to South Beach.**

F

**TINTAGEL**

**Souvenir shop**
**open 8 a.m. – 10 p.m.**

Is this the castle where King Arthur was born? Many people believe so – come and see for yourself. The mystical atmosphere of these ancient stones is home to the ghosts of legends and myths, the castle sits high above the crashing of the Atlantic ocean upon the crumbling stones of England's coast ...

G

## Milton Keynes is home to this year's Special Summer School

Our town is proud to be host this year to the Special Summer School – the nation's most effective holiday educational programme for children with learning difficulties. Children who attend are accommodated on campus, where activity groups work their way through projects and modules based on the school curriculum. Special extra courses in maths and English are available on request.
Please go to www.sss.mk.co.uk for more information on reservations and courses.

H

## ENO English National Opera

Britain's most famous opera house presents a special summer performance of Leoš Janáček's opera **The Cunning Little Vixen**.The fascinating opera by the Czech composer is one of the most exciting productions in our programme this year – please book in advance as we expect all performances to be sold out!

**Bookings can be made by phone, e-mail, in person, or via the booking form on our website. See below for more details.**

| 5 | 6 | 7 | 8 | 9 |
|---|---|---|---|---|
| | | | | |

### Part 3

*After reading the text, decide if the statements are true or false.*
*Tick (✓) **A** for **true** and **B** for **false**. Mark the correct letter on your answer sheet.*

| | A | B |
|---|---|---|
| 10. Most people are not interested in what their stars have to tell them about their future. | ☐ | ☐ |
| 11. A lot of people are embarrassed to say that they're interested in astrology. | ☐ | ☐ |
| 12. It would be hard to find a magazine that didn't have a regular column about astrology. | ☐ | ☐ |
| 13. The astrology industry makes about one hundred million dollars worldwide each year. | ☐ | ☐ |
| 14. Hardly anyone can make a living as an astrologer. | ☐ | ☐ |
| 15. President Reagan's belief in astrology was an issue that worried a lot of people. | ☐ | ☐ |
| 16. There are about 66 million Americans who don't believe that there is any scientific basis to astrology. | ☐ | ☐ |
| 17. The scientific foundations of astrology have only rarely been proved. | ☐ | ☐ |
| 18. There are more than a million books on the subject of astrology available. | ☐ | ☐ |
| 19. One thing your horoscope claims to be able to tell you is how your love life will develop in the future. | ☐ | ☐ |

**Astrology**

Do you know which star sign you are? Do you care? How often do you read your horoscope? Honestly, now … Most of us have at least a little interest in astrology, even if we don't necessarily believe everything about it, and most of us wouldn't even admit to that little bit of interest in public. But a glance at any newspaper and any magazine will show that most people must be interested – because they all contain horoscopes and astrological information. This industry brings in about $ 100 million in the US alone, and there are an estimated 10,000 full-time and 175,000 part-time astrologers working in the country.

There are a lot of people who never make any important decisions without consulting astrologers – one of the famous examples being the former US President, Ronald Reagan. The American magazine *Time* published an article about his belief in astrology in 1988, which got the President into a lot of trouble – he was widely criticised for letting something as 'weird' as astrology have an influence on the decisions he made as President. But however seriously people may take it or not, astrology is here to stay. Surveys claim that 39 % of adult Americans – that's roughly 66 million people! – believe that there is a scientific basis to astrology. There has never been any successful scientific proof that there is any basis in fact to astrology. But that hasn't stopped people from producing and consuming great amounts of material on the subject (at the moment over 1,000,000 books are available), and it doesn't stop most of us from sneaking a look at the horoscopes in the magazines in the doctor's waiting rooms – will we be lucky in love this month? Should we be careful at work?

## Part 4

*After reading the text, answer the questions below.*
*Mark the correct letter (A–D) on your answer sheet.*

# Alcatraz Holiday Package

**Come to San Francisco** and experience all that Alcatraz offers. This is the site of the first lighthouse and US fort on the west coast of America, as well as being the home of the world-famous prison. When you're here, you can also enjoy the island's natural attractions – visit its gardens, tide pools and wonder at the spectacular views of the bay. You will live in the newly-constructed **Holiday Inn Express Hotel & Suites Fisherman's Wharf**, located within walking distance of the Alcatraz Ferry and the historic San Francisco Cable Cars.

**The Alcatraz package includes:**
- **A stay at the Holiday Inn Express Hotel & Suites Fisherman's Wharf**
- **Alcatraz Cruises – boat trips to and around the island**
- **Alcatraz Tour – a guided tour through the legendary prison**

**Explore the Island!**
Step back in time and experience this legendary island. Through its long history, it has been a fort during the Civil War, a military prison, and one of the most notorious federal prisons in US history. This memorable tour includes: a **45-minute audio presentation** called 'Doing Time: The Alcatraz Prison Tour,' featuring prison guards and prisoners who lived and worked on the island; a video guide and historical documentary; walks through the historic gardens; and a chance to see the island's wildlife.

Alcatraz and history go hand in hand. Once home to some of America's most dangerous criminals, the federal prison that operated here from 1934 to 1963 gave "the Rock" a dark, mysterious and dangerous aura. The presence of infamous criminals like Al "Scarface" Capone, America's most famous gangster, helped to establish the island's legendary reputation.
To this day, Alcatraz is best known as one of the world's most legendary prisons. Many people, though, are unaware of the wealth of other history on the island. Alcatraz is now home to rare flowers and plants, wildlife on land and in the waters of the bay, and thousands of sea birds. Civil War-era buildings across the island give insight into the 19th century, when the island served as both a defence fort and a military prison. You can also see remains of the American Indian Occupation that started in 1969 after the prison closed, marking an important event in the history of the American Indian rights movement.

**Come experience the beauty, history and infamy of Alcatraz on the San Francisco Bay. You'll be surprised by what you learn and see.**

20. Alcatraz is …

**A** ☐ a modern prison for dangerous criminals.

**B** ☐ a nature reserve for endangered sea birds.

**C** ☐ a museum for the American Civil War.

**D** ☐ an island which was the site of a prison.

21. If you take the Alcatraz Package Tour, you will be staying …

**A** ☐ in specially furnished cells in the old prison.

**B** ☐ in a hotel built on the island.

**C** ☐ in a new hotel complex built near the ferry and cable car.

**D** ☐ in the old prison guards' rooms.

22. The audio guide to the prison includes …

**A** ☐ commentary by Al "Scarface" Capone.

**B** ☐ commentaries by Native Americans.

**C** ☐ a guide to the sea birds that can be seen from the prison's windows.

**D** ☐ commentaries by prisoners and by people who had worked on the island.

23. After 1969, what happened to the prison?

**A** ☐ It was occupied by Native Americans who were campaigning for their rights.

**B** ☐ It was destroyed and a new prison was built.

**C** ☐ It became a luxury hotel for tourists in San Francisco.

**D** ☐ It became a museum dedicated to Al "Scarface" Capone, America's most famous gangster.

24. Choose the correct summary of the text.

**A** ☐ The text is an encyclopaedia entry describing the history and features of the island called Alcatraz.

**B** ☐ This is a text written by activists who are angry at the way criminals were treated by the American government during the 20th century.

**C** ☐ The text is for tourists and gives a brief introduction to what is interesting about the island of Alcatraz.

**D** ☐ The text is a guide to the tourist sights and wildlife in and around the San Francisco Bay, and includes a brief mention of the island of Alcatraz.

## Part 5

*Read the text below. To fill in the gaps decide which of the words in the list below fits best. Mark the correct letter on your answer sheet. There is an example at the beginning (0).*

My name is Pwyll, which is (0) _________ for "Paul". I'm living in Botswana, and this is my blog about being an immigrant from Wales in an African country. I came here about six months ago to work as a water supply systems (25) _________, a fancy term meaning I spend most of my time watching videos of pipes to make sure they're all undamaged and in good condition. When I'm not watching the videos, I'm crawling around on hands and knees looking at the pipes myself. But don't stop reading already, (26) _________ that I'm just another European complaining (27) _________ life in Africa, because I do actually enjoy my job; and this is a great place to live. Botswana is one of the countries with the (28) _________ "happiness" rating in the world. You may know a little about it already from the famous novels by Alexander McCall Smith, the Ladies' First Detective Agency? No? Well, they're fun books, I can (29) _________ them. Anyway, (30) _________ I was saying: I've been here for about six months, and I made friends here really quickly – more quickly than a Welshman normally would in London, for example! I only got my Internet connection (31) _________ yesterday, and this is my first blog to say 'hello', but there will be (32) _________ to come. In the future I want to tell you more about the countryside here and the people I've (33) ______, and as I learn it myself, I want to also share more of the history and culture of Botswana. So bookmark this page, and keep (34) ______!

| | | | | | | | | | | | | |
|---|---|---|---|---|---|---|---|---|---|---|---|---|
| 0 | **A** | ☐ | Wales | **B** | ☐ | Whales | **C** | ☑ | Welsh | **D** | ☐ | Welch |
| 25 | **A** | ☐ | technician | **B** | ☐ | technical | **C** | ☐ | technique | **D** | ☐ | technologist |
| 26 | **A** | ☐ | thinks | **B** | ☐ | thought | **C** | ☐ | thinking | **D** | ☐ | think |
| 27 | **A** | ☐ | about | **B** | ☐ | on | **C** | ☐ | for | **D** | ☐ | that |
| 28 | **A** | ☐ | lowest | **B** | ☐ | big | **C** | ☐ | small | **D** | ☐ | highest |
| 29 | **A** | ☐ | recommend | **B** | ☐ | read | **C** | ☐ | enjoy | **D** | ☐ | love |
| 30 | **A** | ☐ | for | **B** | ☐ | because | **C** | ☐ | to | **D** | ☐ | as |
| 31 | **A** | ☐ | instilled | **B** | ☐ | installed | **C** | ☐ | instated | **D** | ☐ | instigated |
| 32 | **A** | ☐ | many | **B** | ☐ | more | **C** | ☐ | lot | **D** | ☐ | amounts |
| 33 | **A** | ☐ | known | **B** | ☐ | meet | **C** | ☐ | got to know | **D** | ☐ | see |
| 34 | **A** | ☐ | reading | **B** | ☐ | learning | **C** | ☐ | watching | **D** | ☐ | blogging |

## Writing

### Part 1

*Below are five sentences spoken during a party: complete the second sentence in each pair so that it means the same as the first sentence.*
*You can use one to three words (and no more than three) to fill in the gaps.*
*There is an example at the beginning (0).*

0. He said to me he'd be here by ten.
   He had ________________ her that he would be at the party by ten.
   *Answer sheet:* 0: told

1. I've never been to a party this good before!
   This is the best party ________________ to!

2. Wow! Martha! You're here too! How long has it been since I last saw you?
   ________________ the last time I saw you?

3. Jenna would only come to the party if we invited Mark.
   After the party: If Mark had been invited, Jenna ________________.

4. If we want to catch the last bus home, we really have to leave now.
   ________________ not leave now, we won't catch the last bus home.

5. It's Erik's party, but he's not having as much fun as everyone else.
   It looks like everyone else is ________________ than Erik.

### Part 2

*Write a short note (of 35–45 words).*

6. You've been invited to stay at a friend's house for the weekend. Confirm that you'll be there and say what you'll be bringing along.

________________________________________________________________

________________________________________________________________

________________________________________________________________

________________________________________________________________

________________________________________________________________

## Part 3

*Choose one of the two tasks 7 or 8 below and write a 100-word text.*
*Indicate which task you have chosen on your answer sheet.*

7. You've probably heard of shopaholics. What do you know about this particular, very modern, condition? And if you haven't heard of them before – what do you think a 'shopaholic' is?

8. Imagine that a friend of yours has entered a talent casting show on TV – and failed miserably … Write an e-mail to your friend trying to comfort them. Remember to be comforting and gentle with your friend!

______________________________________________

______________________________________________

______________________________________________

______________________________________________

______________________________________________

______________________________________________

______________________________________________

______________________________________________

______________________________________________

______________________________________________

# Listening

## Part 1

Track 13

*Listen to the short dialogues. Tick (✓) the correct picture.*
*There is an example at the beginning (0).*

0. What did they use during the power cut?

**A** ☐

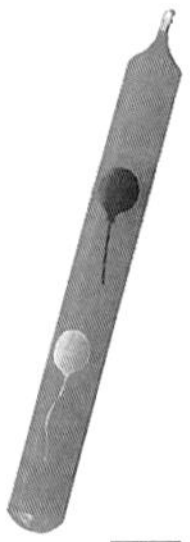

**B** ☐

**C** ☑

1. When is the opening film showing?

A ☐

B ☐

C ☐

2. What item from the shopping list was forgotten?

A ☐

B ☐

C ☐

3. How will they be travelling to visit their aunt?

A ☐

B ☐

C ☐

4. How much does the audio book cost?

A ☐

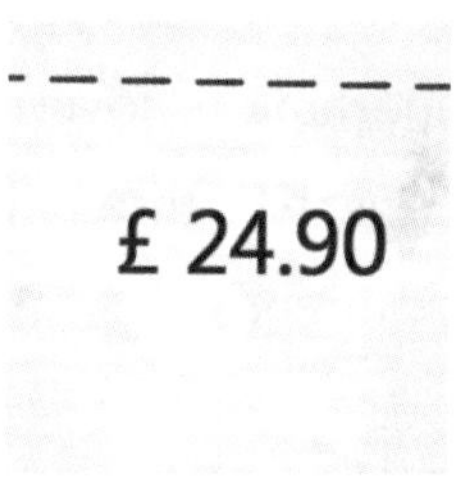


B ☐

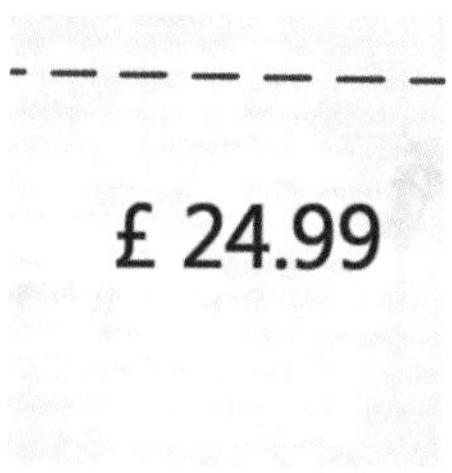


C ☐

5. When does the teacher want to have the pupils' homework?

A ☐

B ☐

C ☐

6. Which sport is on offer at the school?

**A** ☐

**B** ☐

**C** ☐

Track 14

## Part 2

*You will hear a radio report about the Darwin Awards.*
*Tick (✓) the correct box and mark A, B or C on your answer sheet.*

7. When were the Darwin Awards first mentioned?
   - **A** ☐ 1995
   - **B** ☐ 1958
   - **C** ☐ 1985

8. Which of the following are a requirement for Darwin Award nominees?
   - **A** ☐ Being a legal adult, not having hurt anybody else, being dead or unable to produce children.
   - **B** ☐ Being an adult, being awesomely stupid and the first to have done something.
   - **C** ☐ The person must have been killed and there must have been a report about it in the media.

9. Who gets nominated for a Darwin Award?
   - **A** ☐ People who have made important discoveries in the study of evolutionary theory.
   - **B** ☐ People who have killed themselves through their own stupidity.
   - **C** ☐ People who cannot have children.

10. How do events have to be confirmed?
   - **A** ☐ By witnesses and/or media accounts.
   - **B** ☐ By video recordings and witnesses from the official Darwin Awards committee.
   - **C** ☐ By signed statements from the nominees themselves.

11. What was the mistake made by the man who wanted to film the skydivers?
   - **A** ☐ He forgot his camera.
   - **B** ☐ He forgot his parachute.
   - **C** ☐ He was too far away to see them.

12. What did the police find surprising about the man who drowned in his kitchen sink?
    **A** ☐ He managed to fit through the kitchen window.
    **B** ☐ He turned the water on when his head was in the sink.
    **C** ☐ He didn't come in through the front door.

## Part 3

Track 15

*You will hear a man talking about his job as a "roadie".*
*Look for the missing information and fill in the gaps in the text.*

**A roadie's job**

"Roadie" is short for: (13) ____________________

Jobs roadies have to do: carrying (14) ______________________________, building stage sets.

Roadies are often highly trained technicians. They are responsible for (15) ____________________

and (16) ____________________.

Others are very good musicians, who (17) ______________________________ *(one aspect).*

Sometimes they get in trouble with the police, because they (18) ______________________________.

## Part 4

Track 16

*Read the statements below.*
*Then listen to the conversation between two employees at J & P Farnham's Office Suppliers.*
*Decide if the following statements are true or false.*
*Tick* ***A*** *for* ***true*** *and* ***B*** *for* ***false****. Mark the correct letter on your answer sheet.*

| | A | B |
|---|---|---|
| 19. The time is 7 a.m. | ☐ | ☐ |
| 20. There was a big order placed by a telephone company. | ☐ | ☐ |
| 21. The man is going to take care of the big order himself. | ☐ | ☐ |
| 22. Three of the companies the people talking get their office supplies from are demanding more money. | ☐ | ☐ |
| 23. The problem is about the boss's son. | ☐ | ☐ |
| 24. The woman wants to get the police involved in their problem. | ☐ | ☐ |

## Speaking

### Part 1

*In the oral exam there are usually two candidates, an interlocutor and an examiner who observes the conversations. In the first part of the exam the interlocutor asks each candidate about personal details, everyday life, hobbies etc. Or else you are asked to talk to each other. Have a look at mock exams 1 and 2 for possible questions.*

### Part 2

*We are going to describe a situation to you both. You'll then both talk to each other to discuss the topic. The topic for this section is: Food.*
*Look at the pictures, and think about what kind of food they show.*
*Talk together and exchange ideas and opinions about what you see in the pictures.*

## Part 3

*Each of you is now going to be given a photograph.*
*Both photographs are of people watching films. I want you both to take a minute to look at the photograph, because you are going to be asked to describe your photographs to each other.*
*Candidate A will start – Candidate B, just listen and then it's your turn.*
*When you're looking at your photographs, think about which words you will need to describe what you see. Think about things like:*

- *How would you describe the groups of people in each photograph?*
- *Does watching a film in this way have to be arranged beforehand?*
- *Is it expensive to watch films in this way?*
- *How completely do you think the audience can get involved in the pictures and the story if they watch films in this way?*

Photograph Candidate A:

Photograph Candidate B:

## Part 4

*Your pictures both showed different ways to watch films. Each of you will now use both photographs to talk briefly about what you think about these ways of watching films – how much the audience in each case is involved in the film; how much they are concentrating on what they are watching; with whom they watch the film and share the experience; how convenient it is to watch films in this way, how much prior arrangement is required, how much it costs, etc. Now discuss.*

# Lösungsvorschläge

## Reading

### Part 1

1. **A** ☐ People find it offensive to drink alcohol here.
   **B** ☑ It is illegal to drink alcohol in public here.
   **C** ☐ Alcohol is free in this area.

2. **A** ☑ Australians don't drive on the right-hand side of the road.
   **B** ☐ You have to bring your own seat belts with you when you go to Australia.
   **C** ☐ You shouldn't drive when you're on holiday in Australia.

3. **A** ☐ You are not allowed to take luggage which is heavier than 20 kg.
   **B** ☐ You can charge extra if your baggage is heavier than 20 kg.
   **C** ☑ You will have to pay extra if you are bringing luggage which is heavier than 20 kg.

4. **A** ☐ If you press the green button, the next train will come; if you press the red button, the operator will come and talk to you.
   **B** ☐ If there's an emergency, press the green button and a train will come and help you.
   **C** ☑ If you press the red button you will be able to talk to the operator.

### Part 2

| 5 | 6 | 7 | 8 | 9 |
|---|---|---|---|---|
| C | F | D | H | A |

### Part 3

| | A | B |
|---|---|---|
| 10. Most people are not interested in what their stars have to tell them about their future. | ☐ | ☑ |
| 11. A lot of people are embarrassed to say that they're interested in astrology. | ☑ | ☐ |
| 12. It would be hard to find a magazine that didn't have a regular column about astrology. | ☑ | ☐ |
| 13. The astrology industry makes about one hundred million dollars worldwide each year. | ☐ | ☑ |
| 14. Hardly anyone can make a living as an astrologer. | ☐ | ☑ |

| | | | |
|---|---|---|---|
| 15. | President Reagan's belief in astrology was an issue that worried a lot of people. | ☑ | ☐ |
| 16. | There are about 66 million Americans who don't believe that there is any scientific basis to astrology. | ☐ | ☑ |
| 17. | The scientific foundations of astrology have only rarely been proved. | ☐ | ☑ |
| 18. | There are more than a million books on the subject of astrology available. | ☑ | ☐ |
| 19. | One thing your horoscope claims to be able to tell you is how your love life will develop in the future. | ☑ | ☐ |

## Part 4

20. Alcatraz is …

**A** ☐ a modern prison for dangerous criminals.
**B** ☐ a nature reserve for endangered sea birds.
**C** ☐ a museum for the American Civil War.
**D** ☑ an island which was the site of a prison.

21. If you take the Alcatraz Package Tour, you will be staying …

**A** ☐ in specially furnished cells in the old prison.
**B** ☐ in a hotel built on the island.
**C** ☑ in a new hotel complex built near the ferry and cable car.
**D** ☐ in the old prison guards' rooms.

22. The audio guide to the prison includes …

**A** ☐ commentary by Al "Scarface" Capone.
**B** ☐ commentaries by Native Americans.
**C** ☐ a guide to the sea birds that can be seen from the prison's windows.
**D** ☑ commentaries by prisoners and by people who had worked on the island.

23. After 1969, what happened to the prison?

**A** ☑ It was occupied by Native Americans who were campaigning for their rights.
**B** ☐ It was destroyed and a new prison was built.
**C** ☐ It became a luxury hotel for tourists in San Francisco.
**D** ☐ It became a museum dedicated to Al "Scarface" Capone, America's most famous gangster.

24. Choose the correct summary of the text.

| | | | |
|---|---|---|---|
| **A** ☐ | The text is an encyclopaedia entry describing the history and features of the island called Alcatraz. | **B** ☐ | This is a text written by activists who are angry at the way criminals were treated by the American government during the 20th century. |
| **C** ☑ | The text is for tourists and gives a brief introduction to what is interesting about the island of Alcatraz. | **D** ☐ | The text is a guide to the tourist sights and wildlife in and around the San Francisco Bay, and includes a brief mention of the island of Alcatraz. |

### Part 5

| | | | | |
|---|---|---|---|---|
| 25 | **A** ☑ technician | **B** ☐ technical | **C** ☐ technique | **D** ☐ technologist |
| 26 | **A** ☐ thinks | **B** ☐ thought | **C** ☑ thinking | **D** ☐ think |
| 27 | **A** ☑ about | **B** ☐ on | **C** ☐ for | **D** ☐ that |
| 28 | **A** ☐ lowest | **B** ☐ big | **C** ☐ small | **D** ☑ highest |
| 29 | **A** ☑ recommend | **B** ☐ read | **C** ☐ enjoy | **D** ☐ love |
| 30 | **A** ☐ for | **B** ☐ because | **C** ☐ to | **D** ☑ as |
| 31 | **A** ☐ instilled | **B** ☑ installed | **C** ☐ instated | **D** ☐ instigated |
| 32 | **A** ☐ many | **B** ☑ more | **C** ☐ lot | **D** ☐ amounts |
| 33 | **A** ☐ known | **B** ☐ meet | **C** ☑ got to know | **D** ☐ see |
| 34 | **A** ☑ reading | **B** ☐ learning | **C** ☐ watching | **D** ☐ blogging |

## Writing

### Part 1

1. This is the best party **I've/I have been** to!
2. **When was** the last time I saw you?
3. If Mark had been invited, Jenna **would have come**.
4. **If we do** not leave now, we won't catch the last bus home.
5. It looks like everyone else is **having more fun** than Erik.

## Part 2

6. Hi,
   Thanks for the invitation, I'll be there on Friday evening. I'll bring some games for the computer and your PlayStation and some DVDs to watch. We'll have a lot of fun. OK, see you soon! *(36 words)*

## Part 3

7. A shopaholic is like any other kind of addict: in order to feel good about themselves and to hide things from themselves, they have to do certain things. But instead of drinking or gambling or taking drugs, shopaholics have to spend money and buy things all the time. Like other addicts, a shopaholic feels really bad and really guilty afterwards. And most of the things a shopaholic buys are useless. They buy clothes or shoes that never get worn, for example, or electronic appliances that are never used. It's a serious problem that requires help, just like alcoholism or drug addiction. *(101 words)*

8. Hi Emily,
   I was very sorry to hear about the casting show. What a shame. I think you were very brave to get as far as you did. Most people wouldn't have the courage or the self-confidence to even try, so well done! I'm sure that the pressure you felt must have had a bad influence on your performance. I know you can sing really well, and that's not going to change just because of one bad day … I look forward to seeing you in school on Monday, and don't be sad about it, it's not the end of the world!
   Bye,
   Sam *(104 words)*

## Listening: Tapescript

Track 13

## Part 1

0. Man: We had a power cut here last night. It lasted almost two hours.
   Woman: Oh, that must have been scary.
   Man: Sort of. We couldn't find any candles, and we didn't have any matches either. So we had no light until we found a torch. And that took nearly two hours to find. The most annoying thing is, we were recording a programme on TV – and of course that's all ruined now.

1. I got the tickets for the film festival. We have two tickets each for the opening film and that documentary you wanted to see. The first film is at half-past seven on Thursday evening and your film is at ten in the morning on Sunday.

2. Man: Did you do all the shopping?
   Girl: Well I forgot to take the shopping list with me, Dad, but I think I got everything. Let me see – milk, butter, coffee, cola, sausages, potatoes, toothpaste, cucumber, carrots, frozen peas … oh.
   Man: What?
   Girl: I forgot to get the eggs.

3. Woman: This weekend I wanted to take the kids to visit Auntie May. Do you need the car?
   Man: Yes, I'm afraid I do. A work thing. I need it Saturday afternoon and Sunday morning, too.
   Woman: Hmm. Well, I guess we could take the bus.
   Man: No, no, take the train. It's much nicer, the kids love travelling by train.

4. Man: Hello, how can I help you?
   Woman: Hello, I'm looking for an audio book of Tolkien's *Lord of the Rings*. Do you have any in stock?
   Man: Our audio book section is over here. Let me see … Yes, we have a fully dramatised BBC version and here is a complete version read by one speaker.
   Woman: The full cast version sounds good. How much is it?
   Man: That's £ 24.99.

5. Your homework for the weekend is going to require you to go to a library. You'll have to do some research on a subject – you can choose the topics from the list I'm handing out now – and what's most important this time is, you have to make a complete and thorough list of all the sources you used in your research. That means I want full notes on the books you used: the titles, the authors, the publishers, when they were published, and page numbers for all the details you use in your reports. Since the library is closed on Saturday, you can finish your research on Monday. Please hand in your homework on Tuesday morning.

6. Girl: They're considering introducing a new sport at my school – Australian Rules Football.
   Man: Oh! Isn't that terribly dangerous?
   Girl: It certainly looks dangerous. It's like rugby, or American Football without the body armour – and at our school we already have American football, soccer, rugby, cricket, basketball, tennis, hockey and I don't know *how* many other sports.

## Part 2

Track 14 Woman: This week's story in our series on bizarre things to have emerged from the Internet is about the Darwin Awards. First mentioned in 1985 in ancient 'usenet' discussion groups, and now a series of successful books, the Darwin Awards are humorous honours awarded to people who make sure the human species will survive – by removing themselves from the gene pool. And what does all this mean?

Man: The awards are named after Charles Darwin, of course, whose theory of evolution changed the way we see ourselves and the world around us. His idea that everything in nature struggles to survive is the joke of the Darwin Awards. The idea of the Awards is simple: they are awarded to people who have either died or become incapable of producing children through their own stupidity. There are five requirements for winning a Darwin Award: the person nominated must be either dead or unable to produce children. The person's stupidity must be unique and sensational – the Awards are not nominated to people who do just stupid things. They have to be *awesomely* stupid. The third requirement is self-selection. Charles Darwin's idea of natural selection was that, put simply, the strongest survive. In the Darwin Awards, self-selection simply means that nominated people must have killed themselves – not someone else. The fourth requirement is that the person be legally adult, and the fifth and last requirement is that the event must be in some way proved to have happened. There either have to be witnesses or reports in the media to confirm the event.

WOMAN: A couple of famous examples of cases which have won Darwin Awards include the man who jumped out of a plane to take photographs of skydivers – without a parachute …

MAN: And a man who jumped through a window on the fifteenth floor of an office building, because he wanted to prove that the window was unbreakable …

WOMAN: And the Austrian man who came home drunk one night, climbed in through his kitchen window, fell headfirst into the kitchen sink, somehow turned on the hot water tap and drowned. Police wondered why he hadn't just used his own front door; his house keys were in his pocket …

## Part 3

Track 15

I'm a roadie. That's short for "road crew" – and we're the people who travel around with rock bands when they're on tour, and do all the work. That's right. The guys on stage get all the money and all the love for jumping around and posing for two hours a day every now and again. And we're the guys who spend all day carrying heavy stage equipment around, building stage sets, making sure the drums are set up properly and the guitars are in tune, we climb up to put the lights where they should be and we take care of security for the bands. No one knows who we are. No one ever recognises us. And almost no one ever says "thank you" – although none of the whole rock and roll circus would be possible at all without us.

Some of us are highly trained professionals – especially the guys who do the fireworks and the lighting for big, spectacular bands like Rammstein or Kiss. Most of the roadies who are responsible for the instruments – the drum techs who set up the drum kits, and the guitar techs who tune and take care of the guitars – are quite often going to be just as good musicians as the guys in the band. The roadies who do the sound at the concerts are also skilled professionals: they have to be familiar with all kinds of different technologies and they have to be able to *immediately* fix technical problems that occur during a concert. The roadies are also the people who get in trouble with the police, because it's the roadies who a lot of the bands will send out to get drugs for them: so it's the roadies who are picked up by the police. It can be a good job, with a lot of fun and a lot of rewarding work, and it can be a complete nightmare – it depends on the band.

## Part 4

Track 16

WOMAN: And so ends another day at J & P Farnham's Office Suppliers, Limited.

MAN: Is it really seven o'clock already?

WOMAN: Indeed it is. Well. What a day.

MAN: Hmm. Good and bad. This afternoon was a bit of a disaster, I must say.

WOMAN: Yes, I'm afraid it was. And the day started off so well, too – that huge order from the telephone company, that makes up three months' average income in one order. Very nice. We'll have to be very careful with that order and make sure *nothing* goes wrong. I'll have to take care of that one myself.

MAN: That certainly was good news. But what are we going to do about the delivery services? Three of the companies we use to deliver our products are demanding more money.

WOMAN: I don't know what to do about that yet. I'd like to tell them all to – well, you know. There are a lot of other companies that could take care of the delivery side of the business for us. But on the other hand, these are people we've worked with for a long time now, it would be in very bad taste to just cut all business contacts to them now. We'll have to try and find some kind of compromise, I think.

MAN: And then we have the problem of the boy doing work experience in the warehouse.

WOMAN: … Ah yes. That is a problem.

MAN: He's the nephew of the boss.

WOMAN: Yes he is.

MAN: And I caught him stealing from the employees' things in the break room. He'd put over £50 in his pockets and had six watches and a whole lot of jewellery, too.

WOMAN: Yes, that's an ugly situation.

MAN: In my opinion we shouldn't make a big deal out of it – return the money and the items, don't contact the police, but take the boy to his uncle and make it clear that something has to be done about it.

WOMAN: I see what you mean, but I would personally rather get the police involved. That little devil needs to be scared right now, before he makes any more stupid mistakes. The police will be able to deal with a situation like this better than the boss will, I promise you that.

## Listening: Solutions

### Part 1

1. When is the opening film showing?

**A** ☑

**B** ☐

**C** ☐

2. What item from the shopping list was forgotten?

 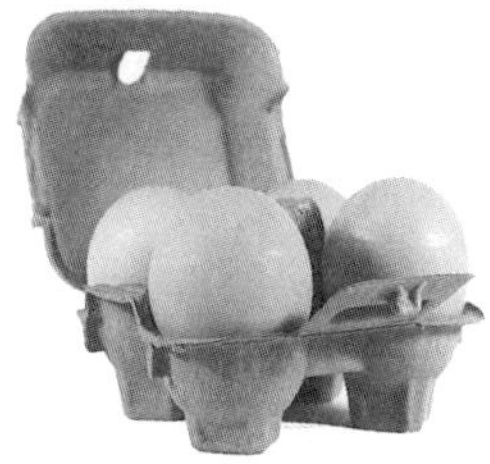 

A ☐ B ☑ C ☐

3. How will they be travelling to visit their aunt?

A ☑ B ☐ C ☐

4. How much does the audio book cost?

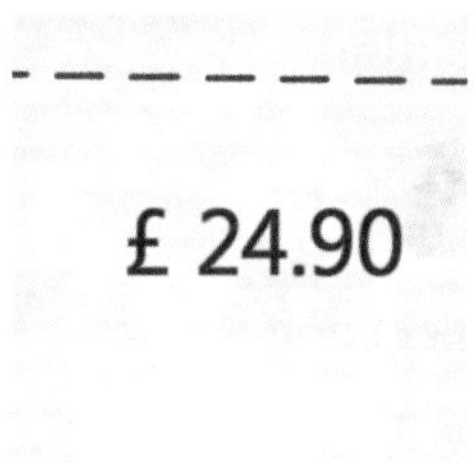

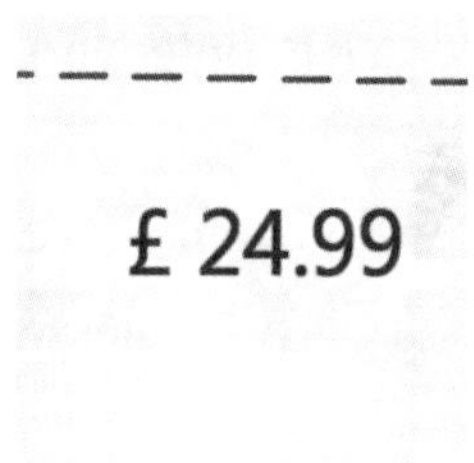


A ☐ B ☐ C ☑

5. When does the teacher want to have the pupils' homework?

A ☑ B ☐ C ☐

6. Which sport is on offer at the school?

A ☑ B ☐ C ☐

## Part 2

7. When were the Darwin Awards first mentioned?
   - **A** ☐ 1995
   - **B** ☐ 1958
   - **C** ☑ 1985

8. Which of the following are a requirement for Darwin Award nominees?
   - **A** ☑ Being a legal adult, not having hurt anybody else, being dead or unable to produce children.
   - **B** ☐ Being an adult, being awesomely stupid and the first to have done something.
   - **C** ☐ The person must have been killed and there must have been a report about it in the media.

9. Who gets nominated for a Darwin Award?
   - **A** ☐ People who have made important discoveries in the study of evolutionary theory.
   - **B** ☑ People who have killed themselves through their own stupidity.
   - **C** ☐ People who cannot have children.

10. How do events have to be confirmed?
    - **A** ☑ By witnesses and/or media accounts.
    - **B** ☐ By video recordings and witnesses from the official Darwin Awards committee.
    - **C** ☐ By signed statements from the nominees themselves.

11. What was the mistake made by the man who wanted to film the skydivers?
    - **A** ☐ He forgot his camera.
    - **B** ☑ He forgot his parachute.
    - **C** ☐ He was too far away to see them.

12. What did the police find surprising about the man who drowned in his kitchen sink?
    - **A** ☐ He managed to fit through the kitchen window.
    - **B** ☐ He turned the water on when his head was in the sink.
    - **C** ☑ He didn't come in through the front door.

## Part 3

**A roadie's job**

"Roadie" is short for: (13) *road crew*

Jobs roadies have to do: carrying (14) *(heavy) stage equipment*, building stage sets.

Roadies are often highly trained technicians. They are responsible for (15) *fireworks* and (16) *lighting*.

Others are very good musicians, who (17) *take care of the instruments / tune the guitars* *(one aspect)*.

Sometimes they get in trouble with the police, because they (18) *buy drugs for the band*.

## Part 4

| | A | B |
|---|---|---|
| 19. The time is 7 a.m. | ☐ | ☑ |
| 20. There was a big order placed by a telephone company. | ☑ | ☐ |
| 21. The man is going to take care of the big order himself. | ☐ | ☑ |
| 22. Three of the companies the people talking get their office supplies from are demanding more money. | ☐ | ☑ |
| 23. The problem is about the boss's son. | ☐ | ☑ |
| 24. The woman wants to get the police involved in their problem. | ☑ | ☐ |

# Speaking

## Part 1

Mögliche Antworten zu diesem Teil findest du in den Lösungen zu *Mock Exams* 1 und 2.

## Part 2

***Hinweis:** Folgende Vokabeln sind für die Bearbeitung dieser Aufgabe hilfreich. Falls du einige davon noch nicht kennst, übernimm sie in dein Vokabellernsystem:*
- *fatty (fett), fattening (dick machend), calories, overweight*
- *quick, cheap, convenient (praktisch), large portion*
- *preservatives (Konservierungsstoffe), additives (Zusatzstoffe), chemicals*
- *clean, fresh*
- *sugar-free, nutritious, healthy, vitamins*
- *environmental issues*

CANDIDATE A: The pictures show different kinds of food. The picture in the middle and the one at the top on the right show food which is healthy and good for you. The other pictures show very unhealthy food.

CANDIDATE B: The healthy food includes fresh fruit and vegetables, juice and cheese. This food is healthy because it provides vitamins and contains things which the body needs to function, in moderate amounts.

CANDIDATE A: And the unhealthy food you can see in the other pictures includes pizza, chips and burgers. This type of food is also called "fast food" or "junk food" – it is unhealthy because it contains high levels of fat and sugar, which are OK for the human body in certain amounts. But in fast food there is usually far more sugar and fat than the human body needs, and these extra amounts make people fat and are bad for their teeth, their blood and their hearts.

CANDIDATE B: You're right, but there are also environmental issues to consider when choosing how to eat – cooking with fresh fruit and vegetables means that you produce very little rubbish. But when you eat fast food all the time, you are constantly producing massive amounts of rubbish because of all the packaging involved.

CANDIDATE A: The problem with the healthy food shown in the picture is that this kind of food is more difficult to prepare for a meal. Unhealthy fast food is convenient, cheap and is very easily available. A lot of food experts say that people need to be better educated about food, because there is a belief – which isn't correct – that it is much more expensive and much more difficult to make healthy meals at home.

CANDIDATE B: No, just as you say, that isn't correct. It is neither more expensive nor more difficult: it just means that you have to think a bit more about what you buy and what you want to eat. The other big problem with fast food full of calories is that it is addictive, due to the high levels of sugar and fat it contains.

## Part 3

CANDIDATE A: My photo shows people who are about to watch a film at the cinema. People are sitting in the audience and waiting for the film to start. One of them has a programme in his hands. Maybe he is already planning his next visit to the cinema. Some of the people have probably bought soft drinks, ice-cream or popcorn. Going to the cinema is of course more expensive than watching a film at home. You also have to plan your visit, and maybe buy or reserve tickets in advance. But the experience of watching the film is different, too. The sound system is much better and more realistic at the cinema. Thus you feel more involved in the action and sometimes get the feeling you are taking part in the film yourself. In my opinion there are some films that are only really good if you watch them at the cinema, for example action films like the James Bond films or films where the soundtrack is very important.

CANDIDATE B: As you said, these pictures show very different ways of watching films. You were right that the first picture, which shows people in a cinema, needs more organization, and that it is more expensive than what we see in my picture, which shows people watching a film on a laptop. I don't think, though, that this way to watch films – on a small computer screen – is at all a good way to enjoy films. It may be quicker, cheaper and more convenient, but it also means that you are constantly distracted by everything around you; the picture is too small for you to see everything clearly; it's hard to get good sound out of a laptop, so the soundtrack in the film is wasted; and it's hard to concentrate for a long time on one computer screen, especially if you're sitting in a tight group with friends. There are, however, also advantages. You can discuss the action of the film with your friends whenever you like and you won't disturb anyone. Or if the film is no good you can quickly decide to watch a different one.

## Part 4

The big advantages of watching a film in the cinema are that you can concentrate on the film and that you can enjoy the full experience of sight and sound. You are sitting in a darkened room, where certain rules of behaviour are expected – you should be quiet during the film and switch off your mobile! And all you are doing is letting the film affect you. The picture is big, the sound is loud and clear, and you have nothing to distract you. You may watch the film together with friends or you might just as well be sitting next to complete strangers. But you're there to watch a film, not to make friends! And yes, it is more expensive than watching a DVD on a laptop, but you are also getting a lot more experience for your money. When you are watching a film on DVD you do not pay attention in the same way as in the cinema. Often you do something else while watching, like doing your homework or tidying up your room.

## Reading

### Part 1

*Read the texts and choose the correct explanation.*
*Tick (✓) the correct sentences and mark the letter (A–C) on your answer sheet.*
*There is an example at the beginning (0).*

0.

- ☑ **A** In 200 yards there will be a place for people to cross the road on foot.
- ☐ **B** In 200 yards only people on foot can use the street.
- ☐ **C** The place where people can cross the road on foot is 200 yards long.

1.

- ☐ **A** Between 10 a.m. and 4 p.m., you can only get into vehicles here.
- ☐ **B** The only vehicles allowed here at night are those entering the building.
- ☐ **C** Only vehicles entering the building are allowed between 10 in the morning and 4 in the afternoon.

2.

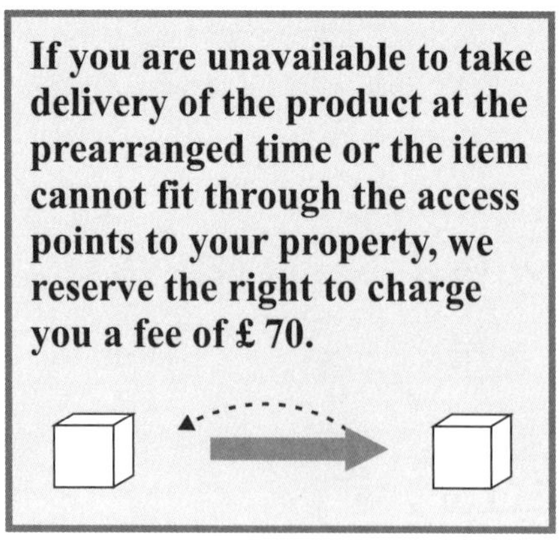


- ☐ **A** If the item you have ordered is too large to be brought into your house, then you have to pay more for the delivery.
- ☐ **B** If you don't help the courier bring the item you ordered into your house, you will be charged extra.
- ☐ **C** If the delivery service doesn't bring your item at the time you arranged, then they have to pay £70.

3.

☐ **A** You can receive the item you ordered by tomorrow morning if you select "Express delivery". But the delivery will not be guaranteed.

☐ **B** To get your delivery by tomorrow you must order soon and select a specific delivery option.

☐ **C** To use the Express option you must order within the next 15 minutes.

4.

☐ **A** In this area the noise will be very loud.

☐ **B** People who are afraid of heights should not enter this area.

☐ **C** On the construction site there will be very nasty smells.

## Part 2

*Match the sentences (5–9) to the pictures (A–H) on the next page.*
*Mark the correct letter on your answer sheet.*

5. Grandpa is in a wheelchair, but even if something happens to him, he can't ring anyone for help in this area.
6. You can leave your car here and continue your journey in another kind of vehicle.
7. Just stand on this and it will take you up to the next floor in this department store.
8. If you don't want to use the stairs, you can get into this and go up or down to the floor you want.
9. Even if you're not fit and active, our water sports facilities are OK for you to use.

**A**

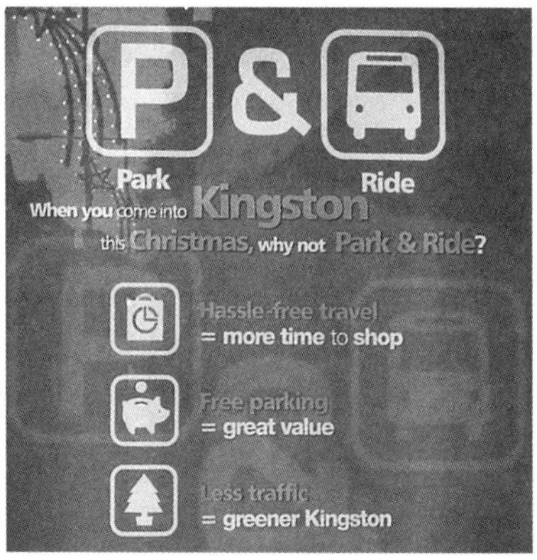


**B**

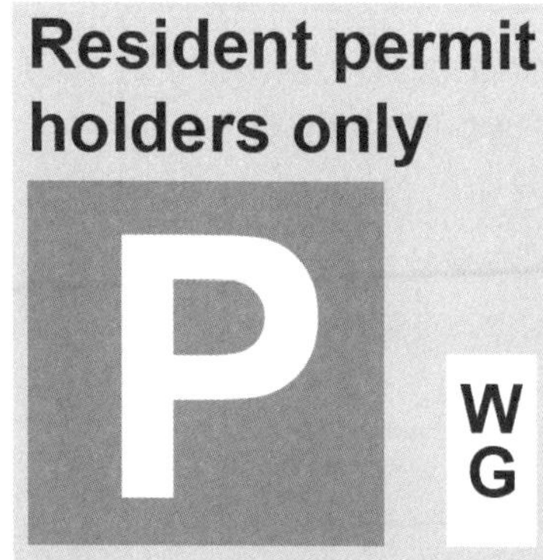


**C**

**D**

**E**

**F**

**G**

**H**

| 5 | 6 | 7 | 8 | 9 |
|---|---|---|---|---|
| | | | | |

## Part 3

*After reading the text, decide if the statements are true or false.*
*Tick (✓) **A** for **true** and **B** for **false**. Mark the correct letter on your answer sheet.*

| | A | B |
|---|---|---|
| 10. Cyberbullying is an old problem in a new form. | ☐ | ☐ |
| 11. Bullies (and cyberbullies) always have the same reason for wanting to hurt other people. | ☐ | ☐ |
| 12. People on the Internet are usually very careful about what they say. | ☐ | ☐ |
| 13. Internet users in online communities are usually paying attention to what other people are doing or saying. | ☐ | ☐ |
| 14. For some people cyberbullying is a form of entertainment. | ☐ | ☐ |
| 15. Among adults, the phenomenon has a different name which is taken from the word "stalking". | ☐ | ☐ |
| 16. The problem of cyberbullying is less worrying now than it was a few years ago. | ☐ | ☐ |
| 17. Most children or young adults who are abused or attacked online will tell their parents about it. | ☐ | ☐ |
| 18. More than a quarter of all victims of cyberbullying don't know who it was who attacked them. | ☐ | ☐ |
| 19. The danger of cyberbullying is that the victims have no way to escape from the abuse. | ☐ | ☐ |

### Cyberbullying

If someone spends time in interactive communities on the Internet – whether they're discussion groups, chat rooms, instant messaging groups or others – and find they're being repeatedly attacked and insulted by another user or users, then they're a victim of cyberbullying. It's a modern form of an old problem. The desire to hurt, offend, embarrass or isolate someone can have different reasons, but the effects are always the same.

One of the features of modern information technology is the anonymous nature of communication: people on the Internet often write and say things they would never dare say in real life. This leads in some cases to an extreme rise in offensive behaviour, because some people think that they can't be caught and punished for what they do or say. And because online communities always involve lots of people who are watching what everyone else is doing, this leads to the growth of cyberbullying as a form of entertainment. But there are still victims.

Cyberbullying is a phenomenon mostly aimed at children or young people; among adults it is even more sinister and potentially dangerous, and is called cyberstalking. But the damage that can be done to the victims of cyberbullying online is no less than the damage that can be done to the victims of bullying in schools. One worrying thing is that the trend towards picking on others online is growing: researchers into Internet and online behaviour say that cases of bullying have been dramatically increasing over the past few years. Nearly 60 % of all children or young adults using the Internet have reported being the victims of abuse from other people online; and the same proportion have also said that they have *not* reported this to their parents. Over 40 % of the victims of cyberbullying don't know who it was who was attacking them.

One major difference between cyberbullying and "traditional" bullying is that the victim can choose not to go to the chat rooms where they have been attacked, and can also choose to ignore or block e-mails or text messages from people they don't know. But this is a lesson that will only be learned after the attacks have started.

## Part 4

*After reading the text, answer the questions below.*
*For each question, mark the correct letter (A–D) on your answer sheet.*

### Déjà vu: The facts?

We all know the feeling: you're walking down the street and you see someone doing something and – what? I've been here before! But how can that be? You know that you've seen this exact scene before now – but that's not possible. Is it?

The feeling is called "déjà vu" – from the French, "already seen". It's one of the most fascinating phenomena we know of, and it's part of one of the most mysterious and unknown abilities we have – our memory. Over 70 % of all adults and children have reported experiencing déjà vu at least once in their lives, and some people experience it frequently. Unfortunately, that's about as far as it goes with "the facts". Scientists have been unable to explore the phenomenon in controlled, laboratory situations, so it's very difficult to study it in any serious way. There are however theories about how and why it happens.

The most simple theory is that it's just a case of our memory playing tricks with us. You see a small child carrying a red balloon, and your brain tells you "Hey! I remember that! You saw exactly the same child with exactly the same balloon, in exactly the same place!" You may even "remember" when you saw it – in a dream two nights ago, or when you were getting off a bus a few months ago. But the theory says: "No. That's simply not true. Your brain is mistaken." Nothing is perfect, of course, and there's no reason to expect our ability to remember things to be perfect (none of us can claim to have perfect memories, can we?). The difference here is that instead of having a hole where something has been forgotten, our brain makes the mistake of thinking that something which we see for the first time is actually being remembered.

Another theory has to do with the nature of how we see things. The idea here is that we look at something, and the information is examined by our brain: but there is a tiny amount of time between the *seeing* and the *thinking* – and in this time the brain makes a mistake. The brain accidentally has two copies of the experience, and the second one seems to be repeating something that is already in the memory.

Another theory is that the things we experience as déjà vu are actually memories of dreams – to follow the earlier example, the small child with the red balloon appeared to you in a dream one time, and now you see it. Which would mean of course that sometimes, the things we dream are things which have not yet happened.

However, these are only theories which try to explain a great mystery which, so far, no one can prove or even study. So it's up to you: the next time you experience déjà vu, you are free to decide for yourself which theory you think best explains what you feel …

20. Déjà vu is found among …

**A** ☐ most adults and children.
**B** ☐ only adults.
**C** ☐ only children.
**D** ☐ only people who are taking strong medicines.

21. Scientists …

**A** ☐ can study déjà vu in controlled environments.
**B** ☐ have learned very little about it.
**C** ☐ know how to cure it.
**D** ☐ don't believe it exists.

22. The first theory about déjà vu is that …

**A** ☐ our brains function too slowly to understand what we are seeing.
**B** ☐ we all have psychic powers.
**C** ☐ we are 'remembering' things which have not yet happened.
**D** ☐ our memory is playing tricks with us.

23. Déjà vu is …

**A** ☐ a serious mental illness.
**B** ☐ a strange phenomenon that no one can explain.
**C** ☐ the French name for the study of memory.
**D** ☐ the theory that we can tell the future in our dreams.

24. Choose the summary below which best applies to the text.

| | | | |
|---|---|---|---|
| **A** ☐ | The text is a scientific study of the nature and causes of the phenomenon known as déjà vu. | **B** ☐ | The text is a humorous parody of scientists' failure to understand the nature of déjà vu. |
| **C** ☐ | The text is about the belief that we all of us have almost magical powers and are able to tell the future. | **D** ☐ | The text is a brief summary of what is known about déjà vu and a look at a few theories about what it may be. |

## Language Elements

*Read the text; the gaps in the text can be filled in using the words in the lists below.*
*For each space (1–10), mark the correct letter (A–D) on your answer sheet.*
*There is an example at the beginning (0).*

**The sad achievement of the UK**

The United Kingdom has (0) _______ the world some wonderful things – a rich history, one of the most sophisticated literary traditions in the world, pop music, (1) _______ play, the telephone, cricket and the (2) _______ of gravity – but today, one of the UK's most noticeable world achievements is that it has one of the highest levels of teenage pregnancies in the world – over 50 cases among 1,000 women, more than double the levels of the (3) _______ of Scandinavia or Asia. (4) _______ the risks and dangers of getting pregnant when you're under 18 are not necessarily physical, the consequences for young mothers' future lives are much more (5) _______. In most cases the pregnancy happens outside of marriage, which can in itself be a cause for concern in many social groups. The chances of a teenage mother completing an education and being in any way prepared for (6) _______ life are very small. Most British teenage mothers officially live in (7) _______ and are unemployed. The effects on the children are easy to guess: being raised in a poor, uneducated environment, the chances are very high that they will also do badly at school, (8) _______ early, fail to get any kind of higher education, and go straight from school into unemployment. The social effects are just as damaging as the economic ones. Living in poverty, young mothers and their children are unable to (9) _______ in a "normal" social life, and will be treated badly and with disrespect by most of the rest of the population. Teenage pregnancy is seen to be one of the major causes of the breakdown of British society, yet it is itself simply a product of certain things which have gone wrong in all developed countries over time, especially the failure to (10) _______ good education – including an understanding of social responsibility – for all members of the population.

| | | | | |
|---|---|---|---|---|
| 0 | **A** ☑ given | **B** ☐ left | **C** ☐ gifted | **D** ☐ presented |
| 1 | **A** ☐ fear | **B** ☐ foul | **C** ☐ fair | **D** ☐ fairy |
| 2 | **A** ☐ discussion | **B** ☐ discover | **C** ☐ discoverer | **D** ☐ discovery |
| 3 | **A** ☐ natives | **B** ☐ nations | **C** ☐ national | **D** ☐ nationalist |
| 4 | **A** ☐ while | **B** ☐ when | **C** ☐ why | **D** ☐ where |
| 5 | **A** ☐ humorous | **B** ☐ serious | **C** ☐ anxious | **D** ☐ numerous |
| 6 | **A** ☐ job | **B** ☐ work | **C** ☐ working | **D** ☐ professionally |
| 7 | **A** ☐ wealth | **B** ☐ London | **C** ☐ poverty | **D** ☐ poor |
| 8 | **A** ☐ drop out | **B** ☐ drop by | **C** ☐ drop in | **D** ☐ fall through |
| 9 | **A** ☐ take up | **B** ☐ take part | **C** ☐ took part | **D** ☐ take some |
| 10 | **A** ☐ provide | **B** ☐ prove | **C** ☐ providing | **D** ☐ provided |

## Writing

### Part 1

*Here are five sentences about cars and transport.*
*Complete the second sentence in each pair so that it means the same as the first sentence.*
*You can use one to three words (and no more than three) to fill in the gaps.*
*There is an example at the beginning (0).*

0. My car was repaired last weekend.
   I _______________ car fixed last weekend.
   *Answer sheet:* 0: had my

1. It would be a good idea to book your train tickets now; it'll be more expensive later this week.
   The tickets will be more expensive later. _______________ book them now.

2. Let's fly to Scotland, it's much quicker than the train.
   It'd be _______________ to take the train, I'd rather fly.

3. We don't have a car anymore; we have to travel by train.
   We _______________ a car but now we have to travel by train.

4. I advise you to book a first class seat for such a long journey; you won't regret it.
   If ______________________________ I'd travel first class; it's more comfortable.

5. Both our children prefer flying to travelling by car or bus.
   ______________________________ children likes travelling by car or bus.

## Part 2

*Write a short text (of 35–45 words):*

6. You have won two tickets for the cinema in a radio competition. Write a brief text message to a friend saying what film you're going to see, when and where it's on, and asking whether they would like to come with you.

________________________________________________________________

________________________________________________________________

________________________________________________________________

________________________________________________________________

## Part 3

*Choose one of the two tasks 7 <u>or</u> 8 below and write a 100-word text.*
*Indicate which task you have chosen on your answer sheet.*

7. Which other countries have you visited, or would you like to visit? Which did you like best, or which interests you most?

8. Use this opening sentence to complete a short story:
   *"The police knocked at our door at eight in the morning ..."*

________________________________________________________________

________________________________________________________________

________________________________________________________________

________________________________________________________________

________________________________________________________________

________________________________________________________________

________________________________________________________________

________________________________________________________________

________________________________________________________________

________________________________________________________________

## Listening

### Part 1

Track 17

*Listen to the short texts. Tick (✓) the correct picture.*
*There is an example at the beginning (0).*

0. Which photo could have been taken at the office this week?

**A** ☐

**B** ☐

**C** ☑

1. Where did the man lose his mobile phone?

**A** ☐

**B** ☐

**C** ☐

2. Which job does the man apply for?

**A** ☐

**B** ☐

**C** ☐

3. Why did the woman not go to the festival?

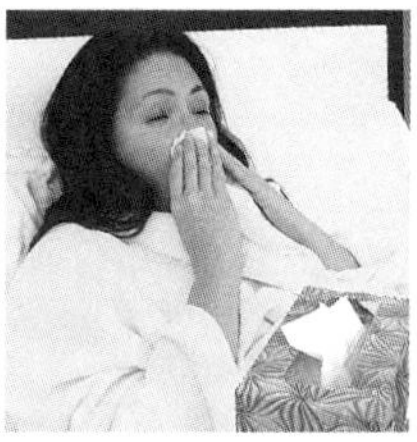

**A** ☐

**B** ☐

**C** ☐

4. Where is the worst weather going to be today?

**A** ☐

**B** ☐

**C** ☐

5. What did Roland Gibson do in the talent competition?

**A** ☐

**B** ☐

**C** ☐

6. What do the man and the woman have for dinner on Saturday?

**A** ☐

**B** ☐

**C** ☐

## Part 2

Track 18

*You will hear an employee of Braddock's Hotel welcome new guests. Tick (✓) the correct box and mark A, B or C on your answer sheet.*

7. Why does the man thank the guests?
   - **A** ☐ Because they have chosen the hotel for their holidays.
   - **B** ☐ Because they have chosen the hotel for their conference.
   - **C** ☐ Because they have been so nice during their stay at the hotel.

8. In front of the hotel, to the left is the …
   - **A** ☐ sauna and sports hall.
   - **B** ☐ swimming pool.
   - **C** ☐ conference room.

9. What do the guests have to do if they get lost in the hotel grounds?
   - **A** ☐ Ask the employees for help
   - **B** ☐ Follow the white stones
   - **C** ☐ Follow the white signs

10. How many rooms are there in the hotel?
    - **A** ☐ 25
    - **B** ☐ 64
    - **C** ☐ Over fifty

11. Which of the dining rooms has been reserved for the members of the conference?
    - **A** ☐ The largest, with the view over the lake
    - **B** ☐ All three
    - **C** ☐ The one closest to the reception desk

12. What extra service has been provided in the conference rooms?
    - **A** ☐ Extra waiters
    - **B** ☐ A private lift
    - **C** ☐ A bar and buffet

## Part 3

Track 19

*You will hear a woman talking about her family's plans for the summer holidays. Look for the missing information and fill in the gaps.*

**Cycling across Europe**

Britain: (13) ____________________ – London – (14) ____________________ Tunnel

France: Paris (staying with (15) ______________________________) – trip through northern France (stopping at (16) ____________________________).

Germany: Cologne – Berlin (visiting friends) – (17) ___________________________ (staying at a hotel)

The hardest part: (18) _____________________________________________

Austria: Salzburg (staying with relatives)

## Part 4

Track 20

*Read the statements below, then listen to the conversation between a man and a woman who are on a shopping trip.*
*Decide if the following statements are true or false.*
*Tick (✓) **A** for **true** and **B** for **false**. Mark the correct letter on your answer sheet.*

| | A | B |
|---|---|---|
| 19. They don't go shopping in London very often. | ☐ | ☐ |
| 20. They have been in five shoe shops already. | ☐ | ☐ |
| 21. The man thinks the shoes are not very nice. | ☐ | ☐ |
| 22. The woman is exhausted and wants to go home after she has bought the shoes. | ☐ | ☐ |
| 23. The man wants to watch the rest of his programme first. | ☐ | ☐ |
| 24. The woman will sit down and wait for him. | ☐ | ☐ |

# Speaking

## Part 1

*In the oral exam there are usually two candidates, an interlocutor and an examiner who observes the conversations. In the first part of the exam the interlocutor asks each candidate about personal details, everyday life, hobbies etc. Or else you are asked to talk to each other. Have a look at mock exams 1 and 2 for possible questions.*

## Part 2

*We are going to describe a situation to you both. You'll then both talk to each other to discuss the topic. The topic for this section is: Communication.*
*Here are some pictures to give you ideas. Look at the pictures, and think about the uses, benefits and disadvantages of the different methods of communication they show. Talk together and exchange ideas and opinions about what you see in the pictures.*

## Part 3

*Each of you is going to be given a photograph. Both photographs illustrate a genre of popular music. I want you both to take a minute to look at the photograph, because you are going to be asked to describe your photographs to each other.*
*Candidate A will start – Candidate B, just listen and then it's your turn.*
*When you're looking at your photographs, think about which words you will need to describe what you see. Think about things like:*

- *What kind of music do you think is performed by the artists in the photographs?*
- *Who does this kind of music appeal to? Do you like the genre?*
- *Do you know anything about the origin of the genre?*
- *What subjects do you think this kind of music tends to cover in its lyrics?*

Photograph Candidate A:

Photograph Candidate B:

## Part 4

*Your pictures both showed artists from two very different genres of popular music. Each of you will now use both photographs to briefly talk about what you think about these styles of music – whether you're familiar with the styles, whether you like either of them, what kind of subjects songs in each genre are about, how popular these styles of music are, etcetera.*
*Now discuss.*

# Lösungsvorschläge

## Reading

### Part 1

1. **A** ☐ Between 10 a.m. and 4 p.m., you can only get into vehicles here.
   **B** ☐ The only vehicles allowed here at night are those entering the building.
   **C** ☑ Only vehicles entering the building are allowed between 10 in the morning and 4 in the afternoon.

2. **A** ☑ If the item you have ordered is too large to be brought into your house, then you have to pay more for the delivery.
   **B** ☐ If you don't help the courier bring the item you ordered into your house, you will be charged extra.
   **C** ☐ If the delivery service doesn't bring your item at the time you arranged, then they have to pay £70.

3. **A** ☐ You can receive the item you ordered by tomorrow morning if you select "Express delivery". But the delivery will not be guaranteed.
   **B** ☑ To get your delivery by tomorrow you must order soon and select a specific delivery option.
   **C** ☐ To use the Express option you must order within the next 15 minutes.

4. **A** ☐ In this area the noise will be very loud.
   **B** ☐ People who are afraid of heights should not enter this area.
   **C** ☑ On the construction site there will be very nasty smells.

### Part 2

| 5 | 6 | 7 | 8 | 9 |
|---|---|---|---|---|
| C | A | E | F | G |

## Part 3

| | | A | B |
|---|---|---|---|
| 10. | Cyberbullying is an old problem in a new form. | ☑ | ☐ |
| 11. | Bullies (and cyberbullies) always have the same reason for wanting to hurt other people. | ☐ | ☑ |
| 12. | People on the Internet are usually very careful about what they say. | ☐ | ☑ |
| 13. | Internet users in online communities are usually paying attention to what other people are doing or saying. | ☑ | ☐ |
| 14. | For some people cyberbullying is a form of entertainment. | ☑ | ☐ |
| 15. | Among adults, the phenomenon has a different name which is taken from the word "stalking". | ☑ | ☐ |
| 16. | The problem of cyberbullying is less worrying now than it was a few years ago. | ☐ | ☑ |
| 17. | Most children or young adults who are abused or attacked online will tell their parents about it. | ☐ | ☑ |
| 18. | More than a quarter of all victims of cyberbullying don't know who it was who attacked them. | ☑ | ☐ |
| 19. | The danger of cyberbullying is that the victims have no way to escape from the abuse. | ☐ | ☑ |

## Part 4

20. Déjà vu is found among …

**A** ☑ most adults and children.
**B** ☐ only adults.
**C** ☐ only children.
**D** ☐ only people who are taking strong medicines.

21. Scientists …

**A** ☐ can study déjà vu in controlled environments.
**B** ☑ have learned very little about it.
**C** ☐ know how to cure it.
**D** ☐ don't believe it exists.

22. The first theory about déjà vu is that …

**A** ☐ our brains function too slowly to understand what we are seeing.
**B** ☐ we all have psychic powers.
**C** ☐ we are 'remembering' things which have not yet happened.
**D** ☑ our memory is playing tricks with us.

23. Déjà vu is …

**A** ☐ a serious mental illness.

**B** ☑ a strange phenomenon that no one can explain.

**C** ☐ the French name for the study of memory.

**D** ☐ the theory that we can tell the future in our dreams.

24. Choose the summary below which best applies to the text.

**A** ☐ The text is a scientific study of the nature and causes of the phenomenon known as déjà vu.

**B** ☐ The text is a humorous parody of scientists' failure to understand the nature of déjà vu.

**C** ☐ The text is about the belief that we all of us have almost magical powers and are able to tell the future.

**D** ☑ The text is a brief summary of what is known about déjà vu and a look at a few theories about what it may be.

## Language Elements

| | | | | |
|---|---|---|---|---|
| 1 | **A** ☐ fear | **B** ☐ foul | **C** ☑ fair | **D** ☐ fairy |
| 2 | **A** ☐ discussion | **B** ☐ discover | **C** ☐ discoverer | **D** ☑ discovery |
| 3 | **A** ☐ natives | **B** ☑ nations | **C** ☐ national | **D** ☐ nationalist |
| 4 | **A** ☑ while | **B** ☐ when | **C** ☐ why | **D** ☐ where |
| 5 | **A** ☐ humorous | **B** ☑ serious | **C** ☐ anxious | **D** ☐ numerous |
| 6 | **A** ☐ job | **B** ☐ work | **C** ☑ working | **D** ☐ professionally |
| 7 | **A** ☐ wealth | **B** ☐ London | **C** ☑ poverty | **D** ☐ poor |
| 8 | **A** ☑ drop out | **B** ☐ drop by | **C** ☐ drop in | **D** ☐ fall through |
| 9 | **A** ☐ take up | **B** ☑ take part | **C** ☐ took part | **D** ☐ take some |
| 10 | **A** ☑ provide | **B** ☐ prove | **C** ☐ providing | **D** ☐ provided |

## Writing

### Part 1

1. The tickets will be more expensive later. **You'd better/You should/I would** book them now.

2. It'd be **too slow / much slower** to take the train, I'd rather fly.

3. We **used to have** a car but now we have to travel by train.

4. If **I were you** I'd travel first class; it's more comfortable.

5. **Neither of our** children likes travelling by car or bus.

### Part 2

6. Hi there,
   I just won some tickets in a radio competition – do you want to come and see the new Batman film at the Odeon in town with me tomorrow night? Let me know!
   Bye *(35 words)*

### Part 3

7. I haven't visited many other countries. I have been to England a couple of times, and also to Scotland, and two years ago I went on holiday to France with my family. I also visited Poland for a weekend to go to a festival, and I went on a cycling tour in Holland last summer. The country I liked most was Scotland: the countryside is so beautiful, and the accent is really wonderful, although Scottish English can be quite hard for a foreigner to understand. The countries I would most like to visit are Canada and Japan – Japan must be very interesting – but very strange! *(105 words)*

8. The police knocked at our door at eight in the morning. My mother was the first person to answer the door – she was pretty frightened when she saw the police officers standing there. "What have you done now?" she screamed at me when I came downstairs just behind her. I was still half asleep – and even more surprised and frightened than she was. "I haven't done anything!" I protested. The policeman at the door smiled. "There's no need to worry, we're just here collecting donations for the police charity fund. Would you like to make a donation?" *(97 words)*

## Listening: Tapescript

### Part 1

Track 17

0. MAN: Did you have a good day at work today, dear?
   WOMAN: Yes, I suppose so. Things were very busy and two of my colleagues were off sick, and since Jenny was fired last month, we haven't really got back into the rhythm yet. I think the rest of this week is going to be quite difficult for Emily and me. We are the only ones in the office. I'll probably be working late tomorrow and Thursday.

1. WOMAN: This is a really nice spot for a picnic. Why don't you call Tim and Helen and ask them if they're free? They'd love it here.
   MAN: Good idea, let me just – oh.
   WOMAN: What's wrong?

MAN: I can't find my mobile. That's odd.

WOMAN: Did you leave it at home?

MAN: I don't think so, I got a text message from Brian when we were in the car on the way here … Oh, no, I hope I haven't left it in the car.

WOMAN: But I thought I saw you put it in your pocket on the way up the hill.

MAN: Damn, you're right. Oh well, I'll have to walk back down and hunt for it.

2. WOMAN: Hello, J & C Media Sales, how can I help you?

   MAN: Hello, my name is Rob Bridges, I'm calling about the job vacancy as a salesman at your shop in the Mill Street shopping centre.

   WOMAN: Mr Bridges, I'm sorry, the vacancy has already been filled. The only vacancy left is that of a caretaker.

3. MAN: Did you have a good time at the festival last weekend?

   WOMAN: Oh, we didn't go in the end. The weather was too bad and my favourite band cancelled their performance, anyway.

   MAN: That's a shame. But you'd bought the tickets already! That's a lot of money to waste.

   WOMAN: My sister still went with her boyfriend, and they found another friend to have my ticket. I went to the cinema on Friday and then spent Saturday and Sunday at my aunt and uncle's farm in the country. My aunt was down with the flu and my uncle needed someone to help him on the farm.

4. Here's the weather report for travellers in Britain today. The south and west is looking forward to some great weather today, lots of sun and summery temperatures. Things get a bit colder the further north we go, and Scotland is going to have to get ready for some stormy weather later today, with strong winds and heavy rains from the Highlands down to Newcastle. The Midlands will be under heavy cloud for most of the day, but the good news is that by tomorrow afternoon the whole country will be under a wonderful June sun, so that'll be a nice weekend for the British Isles for a change.

5. Here are the results of our school talent competition: the third prize is awarded to Chris White with his spectacular display of break dancing. Second place goes to Sharon Wilkins, for her beautiful performance of the theme song from Titanic. And the first prize goes to Roland Gibson, who managed to eat 65 hot dogs in less than two minutes! What an achievement!

6. WOMAN: What shall we have for dinner at the weekend?

   MAN: I fancy some roast beef, actually.

   WOMAN: We can't eat roast beef all weekend. How about if I make a nice salad on Saturday, and we have a big roast dinner on Sunday?

   MAN: Aha. And what about our vegetarian daughter, and her vegan boyfriend?

   WOMAN: Hmm. Well, they can always finish off the rice and tofu, I suppose.

## Part 2

Track 18

Good morning, and welcome to Braddock's Hotel. We're delighted to welcome you all, our guests, for this beautiful weekend. I would like to take this opportunity to thank you for having chosen our hotel as the venue for your annual conference. Now, if you'll follow me, I shall take you on a brief tour of the hotel and its grounds. The hotel is of course the striking building you can see ahead of you; to the left we have the sauna and sports hall, and to the right are the tennis courts and the swimming pools. The path we are following is marked by the white stones along the edges, and can be followed around the entire area of the hotel's grounds. You don't need to worry about getting lost, just follow the white stones! Now, if you'll follow me up the steps, here we are in the hotel foyer. Braddock's has four floors and a total of 52 rooms, including family rooms and the Imperial suites on the top floor. Our dining area is here to the left – there are three rooms, and the largest, there to the rear of the building with the view over the lake, has been reserved for members of your conference. You will find the menu for meals for the weekend in the folders that you were given when you arrived. The lifts are here next to the reception desk, and there are two flights of stairs leading to the upper floors. On the first floor you will find our conference rooms. All three of them have been reserved for you this weekend, and a bar and a buffet has been set up in the largest of the three for your refreshment over the next few days. Now, if you have any questions or wishes, please don't hesitate to ask a member of staff. On behalf of Braddock's hotel, I would very much like to welcome you once again, and wish you a happy, comfortable and successful stay for your conference.

## Part 3

Track 19

Our family holiday this year is going to be quite an adventure. We decided to go as a family, with all three kids, and do a bicycle tour from France through to Austria. We first have to ride from Bristol across to London, where we will take the Channel Tunnel to the European mainland. From there we will ride to Paris, where we will stay for a few days with some old friends of the family. We are bringing tents with us, and from Paris we will take a leisurely trip across northern France, stopping at camp sites along the way, until we get to Germany. We'll be staying with friends in Cologne and Berlin, and then heading down to Bavaria for a week at a hotel near the Wolfgangsee. I'm sure we'll all be very glad of the break there, that'll be a long distance we'll have covered by then! When we leave the hotel, we'll have the hardest part of our trip ahead of us – crossing the Alps into Austria. Once we get there we'll be staying with my sister and her family in Salzburg. My husband wants to travel by train to Vienna to visit an old student friend of his, and then we'll have to see about getting home again. There's a good chance that we'll just pack our bikes and camping gear onto a train and take the easy way home ... but we'll all be very fit by the time we get back home, that's for sure.

## Part 4

Track 20

MAN: OK, this is the longest shopping trip we've ever done.

WOMAN: I know, I know. But I'm nearly finished. We don't get to go to London very often, I thought we should make the most of it.

MAN: I'm getting tired, I must say.

Woman: Look at those shoes! Oh, I must try them on.
Man: Great, another shoe shop. Is this the fifth? Sixth? I've lost count already.
Woman: Don't exaggerate. It's the fourth. Oh, they're lovely … I'll just go and see if they have them in my size. Why don't you – oh, I don't know, find something to do.
Man: There's a television over there. A bunch of kids are watching cartoons. I'll be waiting there, OK? Take your time. *(pause)*
Woman: Aha, here you are. I was looking everywhere for you.
Man: I did say I would be here. Now be quiet, this is really exciting.
Woman: I got the shoes. I'm hungry. Can we go and have lunch now?
Man: Shhh! I want to see what happens next.
Woman: You can't be serious! I've been walking around all day, I'm exhausted and starving, and now I have to wait for you while you watch the Teletubbies?
Man: Please, be quiet! Just be patient. It's nearly over.
Woman: You have to be joking. I can't believe this.
Man: Just five more minutes.
Woman: Well, I'll be across the street in that café when you're finished. Have fun.

## Listening: Solutions

### Part 1

1. Where did the man lose his mobile phone?

**A** ☐ **B** ☐ **C** ☑

2. Which job does the man apply for?

**A** ☐ **B** ☑ **C** ☐

3. Why did the woman not go to the festival?

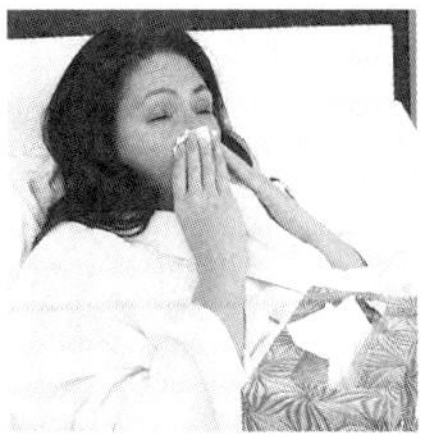

A ☐

B ☐

C ☑ (✓)

4. Where is the worst weather going to be today?

A ☑ (✓)

B ☐

C ☐

5. What did Roland Gibson do in the talent competition?

A ☐

B ☑ (✓)

C ☐

6. What do the man and the woman have for dinner on Saturday?

A ☑ (✓)

B ☐

C ☐

## Part 2

7. Why does the man thank the guests?
   - **A** ☐ Because they have chosen the hotel for their holidays.
   - **B** ☑ Because they have chosen the hotel for their conference.
   - **C** ☐ Because they have been so nice during their stay at the hotel.

8. In front of the hotel, to the left is the …
   - **A** ☑ sauna and sports hall.
   - **B** ☐ swimming pool.
   - **C** ☐ conference room.

9. What do the guests have to do if they get lost in the hotel grounds?
   - **A** ☐ Ask the employees for help
   - **B** ☑ Follow the white stones
   - **C** ☐ Follow the white signs

10. How many rooms are there in the hotel?
   - **A** ☐ 25
   - **B** ☐ 64
   - **C** ☑ Over fifty

11. Which of the dining rooms has been reserved for the members of the conference?
   - **A** ☑ The largest, with the view over the lake
   - **B** ☐ All three
   - **C** ☐ The one closest to the reception desk

12. What extra service has been provided in the conference rooms?
   - **A** ☐ Extra waiters
   - **B** ☐ A private lift
   - **C** ☑ A bar and buffet

## Part 3

**Cycling across Europe**

Britain: (13) *Bristol* – London – (14) *Channel* Tunnel

France: Paris (staying with (15) *old friends of the family*) – trip through northern France

(stopping at (16) *camp / camping sites*).

Germany: Cologne – Berlin (visiting friends) – (17) *Bavaria / Wolfgangsee* (staying at a hotel)

The hardest part: (18) *crossing the Alps*

Austria: Salzburg (staying with relatives)

## Part 4

| | A | B |
|---|---|---|
| 19. They don't go shopping in London very often. | ☑ | ☐ |
| 20. They have been in five shoe shops already. | ☐ | ☑ |
| 21. The man thinks the shoes are not very nice. | ☐ | ☑ |
| 22. The woman is exhausted and wants to go home after she has bought the shoes. | ☐ | ☑ |
| 23. The man wants to watch the rest of his programme first. | ☑ | ☐ |
| 24. The woman will sit down and wait for him. | ☐ | ☑ |

# Speaking

## Part 1

Mögliche Antworten zu diesem Teil findest du in den Lösungen zu *Mock Exams* 1 und 2.

## Part 2

CANDIDATE A: The pictures show different ways of communicating. The oldest and most personal form shown is talking.

CANDIDATE B: The most modern method shown is also the most impersonal – communicating by computer. The smoke signals shown in the picture at the bottom on ther right are also very impersonal, and this is also the most ineffective form of communication.

CANDIDATE A: All the other methods shown allow you to express ideas and discuss things in as much detail as you want, but smoke signals are very limited. The slowest method shown is the post.

CANDIDATE B: Yes, it takes a long time to write a letter, and it can take even longer for the letter to get to the person you are writing to.

CANDIDATE A: But this method also means that you have to put a lot of thought into what you want to say, and how you want to say it. The method of communication that annoys me most is text messages. Whenever I am together with friends everyone is constantly checking their messages or writing messages. It can really get on your nerves.

CANDIDATE B: I think text messages are a very useful modern means of communication. You can pass on information very quickly.

CANDIDATE A: I guess each of these methods has advantages and disadvantages – even smoke signals are good if you are stuck somewhere where there is no post, no computers, and no one close you can talk to.

## Part 3

CANDIDATE A: My photo shows someone who is probably a fan or an artist of black metal or some form of punk or Goth music. Black metal and most punk and Goth music normally appeals to white people who are rebellious in some way. The music and its fashion and attitudes have a lot to do with separating yourself from the mainstream and expressing a "darker" view of life. The music and style can be very aggressive and also very self-involved. I'm not sure but the person in the picture could be the American musician Marilyn Manson – a very controversial person who has often been blamed for being a bad influence on children.

CANDIDATE B: The two photos show people who are fans or artists of very different musical genres. The first photo shows someone who is probably into black metal or some form of punk or Goth music, and the second photo shows what are obviously rappers. Their caps, sunglasses and loose-fitting clothes are typical of people who are into this kind of music. The two people in the picture are probably artists, as you can read the words "MTV Music Awards" in the background. Maybe they have just won an award. In contrast to punk and Goth music, rap and hip-hop are mostly black music, even though the audience is also largely white. Rap and hip-hop, like punk, have their roots in social issues, but unlike punk music the origins lie entirely in the black culture. Personally, I prefer hip-hop to punk and Goth music, because it is more sociable music – more people like it and it is not only about the way that you feel and how much you hate your parents.

## Part 4

I am a big fan of punk and black metal music and I really don't like hip-hop. I know that hip-hop and rap music were very important in black culture from their origins in the 1970s up until the early 1990s, but after that it became just mainstream music and had nothing more to say about social issues or problems. Rap today is only about jewellery and money and sex. Punk music has always been about rebelling against social injustice and being an individual, so it will always be relevant. Punk music can be used by people in the mainstream, but it will itself always be an underground culture. Black metal is even more radical, and is about anti-Christian, antisocial attitudes and usually expresses a deep hatred of society in general and human beings in particular. This is quite entertaining to listen to, but I don't actually believe that everyone who plays or listens to black metal is a Christian-hater and someone who wants to destroy all of society. The rebelliousness and social awareness of punk makes it the most important musical genre illustrated by these two photos.

# Ideal zum selbstständigen Lernen in der 7. bis 10. Klasse

## Englisch Training

- Schülergerecht aufbereiteter Lernstoff mit anschaulichen Beispielen, abwechslungsreichen Übungen und erklärende Lösungen zum selbstständigen Lernen zu Hause.
- Schließt Wissenslücken und gibt Sicherheit und Motivation durch Erfolgserlebnisse.

### Grundwissen Hauptschule

Englisch Grundwissen 9. Klasse ............. Best.-Nr. 93451
Englisch Hörverstehen 9. Klasse mit CD ... Best.-Nr. 93452

### Grundwissen Realschule

Englisch Grundwissen 7. Klasse Realschule ............................. Best.-Nr. 914510
Englisch Grundwissen 8. Klasse ............ Best.-Nr. 90508
Englisch Grundwissen 9. Klasse ............ Best.-Nr. 90509
Englisch Grundwissen 10. Klasse ........... Best.-Nr. 90510
Englisch Grundwissen Übertritt in die Oberstufe....................... Best.-Nr. 82453
Textproduktion 9./10. Klasse ................ Best.-Nr. 90541
Hörverstehen 10. Klasse mit CD ............ Best.-Nr. 91457
Systematische Vokabelsammlung .......... Best.-Nr. 91455

### Grundwissen Gymnasium

Englisch Grundwissen 8. Klasse (G8)....... Best.-Nr. 90508
Englisch Grundwissen 9. Klasse (G8)....... Best.-Nr. 90509
Englisch Grundwissen 10. Klasse (G8)..... Best.-Nr. 90510
Englisch Grundwissen Übertritt in die Oberstufe (G8)............... Best.-Nr. 82453
Textproduktion 9./10. Klasse (G8) ........ Best.-Nr. 90541
Hörverstehen 10. Klasse mit CD (G8) ..... Best.-Nr. 80457
Leseverstehen 8. Klasse (G8)................. Best.-Nr. 90522
Leseverstehen 10. Klasse (G8)............... Best.-Nr. 90521
Wortschatzübung Mittelstufe (G8).......... Best.-Nr. 90520
Englische Rechtschreibung 9./10. Klasse (G8)................................ Best.-Nr. 80453

## Ratgeber für Schüler

Die Ratgeber bieten wertvolle Tipps und Tricks für dauerhaften Lernerfolg.

Richtig Lernen – Tipps und Lernstrategien 7. – 10. Klasse .................................... Best.-Nr. 10482

## Englisch Kompakt-Wissen

Prüfungsrelevantes Wissen in Kompaktform – die prägnante Gedächtnisstütze. Im praktischen Taschenbuchformat.

Englisch Themenwortschatz Hauptschule Best.-Nr. 934501
Englisch Grundwortschatz Hauptschule .. Best.-Nr. 934502
Englisch Themenwortschatz Realschule .. Best.-Nr. 914501
Englisch Grundwortschatz .................... Best.-Nr. 90464
Englisch Kurzgrammatik ...................... Best.-Nr. 90461

## Englisch Lektüre

Stark-Lektüren sind sprachlich den Kenntnissen der jeweiligen Klassenstufe angepasst. Mit Worterklärungen in deutscher Sprache.

Liam Cleary: Echoes and Other Short Stories 7. – 10. Klasse .................................... Best.-Nr. 250008
Rainer Jacob: Abenteuergeschichten 1 7. – 10. Klasse .................................... Best.-Nr. 80454

(Bitte blättern Sie um)

19-SZE